EQUIP. Leadership Series

COURAGEOUS
LEADERSHIP
WORKBOOK

JOHN C. MAXWELL AND EQUIP.

Published by
THOMAS NELSON™
Since 1798
www.thomasnelson.com

Published in Nashville, Tennessee, by Thomas Nelson. Thomas Nelson is a
trademark of Thomas Nelson, Inc.

Published in association with Yates & Yates, LLP, Attorneys and Counselors,
Orange, California.

Thomas Nelson, Inc. titles may be purchased in bulk for educational,
business, fundraising, or sales promotional use. For information, please e-mail
SpecialMarkets@thomasnelson.com.

Scripture references are from the following sources:

THE HOLY BIBLE, NEW INTERNATIONAL VERSION®. NIV®.
Copyright © 1973, 1978, 1984 by International Bible Society. Used by
permission of Zondervan. All rights reserved.

The New King James Version (NKJV), copyright © 1979, 1980, 1982, Thomas
Nelson, Inc., Publishers.

The Message (MSG), copyright © 1993. Used by permission of NavPress
Publishing Group.

NEW AMERICAN STANDARD BIBLE®, Copyright ©1960, 1962, 1963,
1968, 1971, 1972, 1973, 1975, 1977, 1995 by The Lockman Foundation. Used
by permission.

The King James Version.

ISBN 10: 1-4185-1786-0

ISBN 13: 978-1-4185-1786-1

Printed in the United States of America
08 09 10 11 VIC 5 4 3 2

Introduction

by Dr. John C. Maxwell

Leadership lifts people. Leadership lifts people from the life they have to the life they *could* have. I have long believed this, even as a young boy growing up watching my dad model leadership in our home, as well as in being a pastor and a college president.

Over the past thirty-plus years, I have practiced leadership firsthand while growing churches and building companies. Now, my greatest joy comes from training others in leadership. And that's why I want to make this leadership training material available to you.

Until now, this leadership training material has only been available in my international endeavors. In 1996, I partnered with a group of trusted friends to launch EQUIP., a non-profit ministry dedicated to equipping Christians worldwide with the leadership skills needed for advancing the Great Commission in their communities, workplaces, and churches. Under the leadership of current President and CEO John Hull, our leadership training has been translated into thirty-five languages and has been taught in over one hundred countries around the world. By March 1, 2006, EQUIP. realized a personal dream of mine by training one million international leaders! And the ministry continues to grow, with a goal to train and equip an additional five million leaders on five continents over the next five years.

The purpose of the Great Commission is to reach people who are far from God and to raise them up to be fully devoted followers of Jesus Christ. But honestly, this goal is not possible

The Great Commission

Then Jesus came to them and said, "All authority in heaven and on earth has been given to me. Therefore go and make disciples of all nations, baptizing them in the name of the Father and of the Son and of the Holy Spirit, and teaching them to obey everything I have commanded you. And surely I am with you always, to the very end of the age."

— Matt. 28:18–20 NIV

without God-anointed spiritual leadership. Thousands of pastors love God, pray faithfully, work hard, and possess deep love and compassion for people—but their churches experience little or no growth. They need training and inspiration to get the mission accomplished.

It is my heart's desire that you and your church succeed in your passion to reach people for Christ, and I want to help you do this by teaching you how to train leaders in your church.

This material is perfect for you if . . .

- You want to develop your people by investing in them personally.

- You want to grow your church.

- You are busy and have little time to write your own leadership training curriculum.

- You want high-quality, proven, field-tested material developed by veteran leaders.

- You want to equip your leaders to excel in their ministries.

How to Use This Material

This leadership kit, *Courageous Leadership*, features two separate tracks of study:

1. The first track is for the pastor, facilitator, or anyone else who will be teaching this material. In this track of study, you should work through the *Courageous Leadership Workbook* in its entirety. The comprehensive material in this workbook corresponds directly with the Courageous Leadership Audio CD found in this kit. Before teaching the workbook lesson to others, listen to each audio lesson

on CD. Each of the twelve lessons addresses Christian leadership in one of the three major facets of leadership development—spiritual formation, skill formation, and strategic formation.

2. This kit also includes a complete line of study crafted specifically for small group use. The Courageous Leadership Small Group Study Lessons can be found on the DVD, which corresponds directly with the Small Group Study Guide found on the CD-ROM. Each of the twelve DVD lessons is about twenty minutes long. As you lead your small group, watch the DVD lesson first as a group, and then go through the Small Group Study questions together for discussion, assessment, and application. The Small Group Study Guide is downloadable and reproducible for your convenience.

Where can I use this material?

This material is perfect for:

- **Key leader groups**

  Key leader groups refer to groups such as the church staff, the local church board, Sunday school teachers, or any other groups essential to your ministry.

- **Teaching venues**

  A teaching venue refers to any number of possible classroom environments. From Sunday and Wednesday night classes to a special seminar on a weekend to a standard Sunday school class, you could offer this material as an elective course to a broad number of people.

- **Outreach opportunities**

  This opportunity is exciting. You could literally open up this leadership training opportunity to business people in your community. Encourage the business leaders in your church to invite their colleagues to attend, and adapt to make a percentage of your illustrations about the home and marketplace, rather than about church situations only.

- **Small groups**

  Small group leaders are always looking for quality material to share in their groups. What better way to lift people up than to teach them about leadership? The twelve-week study is perfect for this format.

- **Christian schools**

  There is growing enthusiasm to get leadership training to young Christians. We are seeing that high schools are interested in leadership being taught to their students.

The above applications can be used in a number of ways or processes and can be very effective. Remember, do what works best for your group. If you have not done much leadership training in the past or have not been consistent, I recommend that you start small and slow and build the process over the course of time. Don't get too hung up in the details of training people a certain way, as there is no "one way." Put your energy and effort into fully engaging your heart and delivering a world-class experience for those going through the material.

What is my timeline for using the material?

There are several different timelines you can use as you go through the material:

- **Weekly sessions for twelve weeks**

  This is the most obvious, but not the only method. Simply select twelve weeks that work best for you, usually in the Spring or Fall.

- **Monthly sessions for one year, or twice a month for six months**

  This is a slow pace, but the advantage is that you can gain great depth and follow-up on many of the concepts explored by going slowly through the material. This method is good for implementing what you learn through practice and application.

- **Two Saturday seminars**

  By teaching six lessons at a time, you can, in two Saturday sessions, train your leaders in this more intensive "fast track" system.

- **A weekend retreat setting**

  Similar to the Saturday seminar, you can take a weekend away and press through the material in a variety of small group and teaching applications.

- **A special summer course**

  Why should summer be a "down time"? Why not offer an impacting course over four Wednesday nights, covering three lessons a night? Your group could meet in someone's home and gather over a potluck dinner.

Again, there are so many possibilities for applying this material to your needs. The sky is the limit!

Three Keys

As you are working through this material in preparation to teach others, remember to:

1. Keep it simple.

Often, there is a tendency to overcomplicate leadership training. Keep it simple. The only wrong way to do it is not to do it at all. In this leadership training, simply listen to the lesson, learn and practice yourself, and teach it to your leaders and aspiring leaders.

2. Stay consistent.

Over-complication leads to breakdown in consistency. If you make it too difficult or cumbersome, you will get frustrated and want to quit. Stay in the game. Think long term. You are working to develop a life practice, not a just a program.

3. Expect results.

This is a key point. Know why you are developing leaders, what they should "look like" (skills, abilities, qualities, and characteristics), and turn them loose—not into busy work but into Kingdom efforts that will make a difference. Expect much and you will receive much.

Getting Started

- Know why you want to develop leaders in your church or organization.

- Pray for God's favor throughout the process.

- Get buy-in from the top 5 percent of your leaders.

- Decide which method you'd like to use for studying the material.

- Organize your dates, times, and places.

- Review and become very familiar with the material.

- Give the leaders or teachers who will do the training adequate time to prepare.

- Cast vision for the process and recruit people you want to participate.

- Get started!

Keep in mind that leadership is best learned in a leadership culture. That means that you yourself must also keep growing as a leader, casting vision for the value of leadership, and providing on-going training.

Remember, hundreds of thousands of people have used this material around the world. It has worked for them—it can work for you!

Table of Contents

Leadership Begins with an Attitude

Lesson 1

Leaders Think and Perceive the World Differently Than Followers Do

For as [a man] thinks in his heart, so is he.
(Prov. 23:7 NKJV)

It is common to assume that leadership is all about skills and techniques. In reality, our leadership begins when we possess the right attitude about our circumstances and ourselves. This is where all change takes place. William James, the father of modern psychology, wrote: "The greatest discovery of my generation is that humans can alter their lives by altering their attitude of mind." Your attitude will determine your action. Your action will determine your accomplishments. Jesus emphasized this principle by teaching that we must get our *heart* in order before we can get our *life* in order. He said that when there are evil treasures in a man's heart, evil emerges. When there are good treasures in a man's heart, good emerges. It's all about what's inside. Real change occurs from the inside out.

Exercise: Write the name of a person you greatly admire. Then write down what it is that causes you to admire that person.

Now, consider the qualities you wrote down. Do they have more to do with attitude, aptitude, or appearance? (Circle one) Can you see how important attitude is?

13

Biblical Principles about Attitudes

1. My attitude as I begin a task will affect its OUTCOME more than anything else.

For as [a man] thinks in his heart, so is he. (Prov. 23:7 NKJV)

In so many situations, the battle is won before the battle has begun. It all has to do with the frame of mind with which we enter the battle. Are we full of faith, hope, and optimism? Or are we negative and doubtful of getting results? This principle was illustrated when Moses sent the twelve spies into the Promised Land. Joshua and Caleb came back with a positive report. The other ten spies returned with a negative report. Their attitude prevailed, and that generation of people never got to enter the land.

Joshua and Caleb	The Other Ten Spies
a. Saw the fruit in the land	a. Saw the problems in the land
b. Saw themselves in God's hands	b. Saw themselves as small and weak
c. Were optimistic about the future	c. Were pessimistic about the future
d. Encouraged stepping out in faith	d. Prevented the people from progress

CHECK YOUR HEART

Attitude Checklist:

• What is my usual attitude at the beginning of a new experience?

• Are there certain new experiences that cause me to feel negative?

- Do these areas help determine my success with God, family, or ministry?

2. My attitude toward OTHERS determines their attitude toward ME.

Give, and it will be given to you. A good measure, pressed down, shaken together and running over, will be poured into your lap. For with the measure you use, it will be measured to you. (Luke 6:38 NIV)

Generally speaking, people are mirrors. They will reflect the attitude of their leader. You must initiate the attitude you want in return. Leaders must understand this to get results. Jesus said, *"And just as you want men to do to you, you also do to them likewise"* (Luke 6:31 NKJV).

Researchers at a major university reported that a person's success on the job is:

- 13 percent due to understanding the product

- 87 percent due to understanding the people

Four Important Leadership Steps with People:

1. Remember their name. Nothing makes a person feel more important.

2. Recognize their potential. Nothing makes a person feel more unique.

3. Request their help. Nothing makes a person feel more useful.

4. Reward their efforts. Nothing makes a person feel more valuable.

EXAMINE THE WORD

15

3. My attitude is the major difference between SUCCESS and FAILURE.

Watch over your heart with all diligence, for from it flow the springs of life. (Prov. 4:23 NASB)

Proverbs reminds us of how important our attitude toward life is. Out of our hearts flow the springs of life. Think about it—you are only an attitude away from victory. An Olympic gold medal winner once said, "I believe the only difference between gold and silver medal winners is their attitude, not their ability."

Proverbs also lists some abominations to the Lord. Consider them for a moment: pride, coveting, lust, envy, anger, gluttony and slothfulness. All are matters of the attitude.

Conversely, a right attitude can make up for what you may lack in resources. Many leaders in the past have accomplished great things without any resources other than a positive attitude of faith.

4. My attitude can turn my PROBLEMS into BLESSINGS.

Have this attitude in yourselves which was also in Christ Jesus, who, although He existed in the form of God, did not regard equality with God a thing to be grasped, but emptied Himself, taking the form of a bond-servant, and being made in the likeness of men. Being found in appearance as a man, He humbled Himself by becoming obedient to the point of death, even death on a cross. For this reason also, God highly exalted Him, and bestowed on Him the name which is above every name . . . (Phil. 2:5–9 NASB)

16

Three Phases of a Problem:

1. Awareness: We have a problem.

2. Evaluation: What went wrong?

3. Choice: This is where attitude steps in!

We can begin dreaming or become disappointed. We can start building or start blaming. We can get busy or get angry. We can conquer or quit. Whether the problem becomes a blessing depends on you more than God. He desires to turn all things into blessings (Romans 8:28). Remember that much of the Bible was written by prisoners, oppressed minorities, and those in captivity. The writers rose above their circumstances.

5. My attitude can give me an uncommon PERSPECTIVE on life.

All things are possible to him who believes. (Mark 9:23b NASB)

A political leader once remarked, "Some people see things as they are and say, 'why?' I look at things that are not and say, 'why not?'"

A shoe salesman was sent to a faraway country, and after a few days, he sent back the message: "Coming home; nobody wears shoes here." Another salesman from the shoe company visited the same country. He wrote back to the home office after a few days: "Send more shoes! Nobody has them yet over here!" It was the same situation, but it was seen from a different perspective. Dr. J. Robert Clinton once remarked, "The primary difference between a follower and a leader is perspective. The primary difference between a leader and an effective leader is better perspective."

EXAMINE THE WORD

6. My attitude is my best FRIEND or my worst ENEMY.

The good man out of the good treasure of his heart brings forth what is good; and the evil man out of the evil treasure brings forth what is evil; for his mouth speaks from that which fills his heart. (Luke 6:45 NASB)

Attitudes create momentum—positive or negative—for your ministry. Leaders know this. Business executives say the most important elements for potential employees are:

- 5 percent availability

- 5 percent adaptability

- 10 percent ability

- 10 percent appearance

- 70 percent attitude

Note the importance of attitude in both leaders and team members. Practicing psychologists list five rules for evaluating people considered for job promotion: (1) ambition, (2) attitude toward policy, (3) attitude toward colleagues, (4) leadership skills, and (5) attitude to pressure on the job.

A survey was taken among customers to discover why they quit buying goods from certain stores. Here are the reasons listed: 1 percent die; 3 percent move away; 5 percent form other friendships; 9 percent cite competitive reasons; 14 percent list product dissatisfaction; and 68 percent make this change because of an attitude of indifference shown to them by an employee.

7. My attitude, not my ACHIEVEMENTS, will give me happiness.

Thus I considered all my activities which my hands had done and the labor which I had exerted, and behold all was vanity and striving after wind and there was no profit under the sun. . . . I know that there is nothing better for them than to rejoice and to do good in one's lifetime; moreover, that every man who eats and drinks sees good in all his labor—it is the gift of God. (Ecc. 2:11, 3:12–13 NASB)

EXAMINE THE WORD

The thoughts in your mind are more important than the things in your life. Too many leaders think if they could just move to a new place or have different circumstances, they would be happy. We call this "destination disease." Leaders must be cured of it.

Personal Evaluation: Have you ever had these thoughts?

- If I could just serve in a different place, I'd be happier.

- If I just knew that person, I'd be satisfied.

- If things were different here, I would be okay.

- If I would not have done that, I'd feel better about myself.

8. My attitude will change when I CHOOSE to change it.

I call heaven and earth to witness against you today, that I have set before you life and death, the blessing and the curse. So choose life in order that you may live . . . (Deut. 30:19 NASB)

ACTION PLAN

Courageous Leadership Workbook

We cannot tailor-make the situations of our life and leadership, but we can tailor our attitudes to fit them before they arrive. Here's how:

- Believe it is not what happens *to* you but what happens *in* you that matters most.

- Stop blaming something or someone else for your attitude.

- Evaluate your present attitudes.

- Recognize that faith is stronger than fear.

- Ask God to fill you with His Holy Spirit.

- Uncover and put in writing a statement of purpose.

- Enlist the help of an accountability partner.

- Spend time with the right people.

- Select a model to follow.

- Consume the truth. Soak yourself in the Scriptures!

TRUTH IN A PICTURE

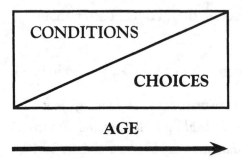

As you mature, life is governed more by your choices than by your conditions or circumstances.

9. My attitude needs continual ADJUSTMENT.

Finally, brethren, whatever is true, whatever is honorable, whatever is right, whatever is pure, whatever is lovely, whatever is of good repute, if there is any excellence and if anything worthy of praise, dwell on these things. (Phil. 4:8 NASB)

Even though the Apostle Paul wrote to mature believers, he still exhorted them to work on their attitudes and watch what filled their minds. Our lives are like sailing a boat or flying a plane. We have a plan for our destination, but there is a need for constant adjustment along the way.

CHECK YOUR HEART

Indicators for Attitude Adjustments

- I have not had enough time with God or myself.

- My family notices and tells me about my attitude.

- My relationship with coworkers becomes strained.

- My view of people begins to lower.

- My perspective on life becomes cynical.

10. My attitude is CONTAGIOUS.

People catch our attitudes like they catch a cold from us—by getting close to us!

Question: What positive attitudes do people catch from you?

_____

_____

_____

_____

21

Courageous Leadership Workbook

ACTION PLAN

Question: What negative attitudes do people catch from you?

_____

_____

_____

_____

_____

ASSESSMENT:

List the top three attitude problems within your church or organization:

1. _____

2. _____

3. _____

Why do you think these attitudes exist within the majority of the people?

_____

_____

_____

_____

How deeply are these attitudes entrenched within the people?

_____

_____

_____

_____

_____

_____

_____

_____

APPLICATION: *Develop a strategy for changing these attitudes:*

- *Model the right attitude for people.*

- *Identify and connect them with leaders.*

- *Disciple leaders in this subject of attitude.*

- *Preach these truths.*

- *Hold people accountable for their attitudes.*

The Leader's Inner Circle

Lesson 2

Building a Healthy Network of Relationships

NOTES

BIBLICAL BASIS

Two are better than one because they have a good return for their labor. For if either of them falls, the one will lift up his companion. But woe to the one who falls when there is not another to lift him up.
(Ecc. 4:9–10 NASB)

Every leader needs relationships in his or her life that provide necessary support and accountability. No man is an island. Building a network of relationships with God and people is a wise step to take toward sustaining your leadership over a lifetime.

Leaders Who Failed

A survey was taken among pastors and Christian leaders who had failed morally. Several hundred pastors were interviewed who had compromised their integrity, fallen into sin, and ultimately lost their ministry. Three consistent observations were made about these fallen leaders:

1. I had stopped spending time alone with **GOD** each day.

2. I had no accountability to **PEOPLE** in my life.

3. I never thought this kind of **FAILURE** could happen to me.

What We All Need

Leaders can avoid pitfalls by establishing and enjoying close relationships with:

- God (your heavenly Father)

- Family (your spouse and children)

- a Paul (a mentor)

- a Barnabas (an accountability partner)

- a Timothy (an apprentice or disciple who follows you)

Why are these relationships especially crucial for a leader? There are several reasons:

- Every leader has **WEAKNESSES.**

- Leaders are on the front line of the spiritual battle and are vulnerable to **ATTACK.**

- Leaders are to set a higher **STANDARD** for themselves than their followers.

- Leaders can be "starving bakers" who are busy **SERVING** bread to others, but never eating for themselves.

- Leaders can be **BLINDED** to the temptations of power and popularity.

- Leaders can get so **BUSY** that their spiritual lives suffer more than anything else.

- Leaders often merely **REACT** to needs and forget to train others for the future.

Your Network

How about you? Do you experience close, accountable relationships in your life? Take a moment and review the following diagram. Do you have people who fill each role?

Write down the names of people who fill each one, then think about whom you might approach for the roles that are empty.

KEY
POINTS

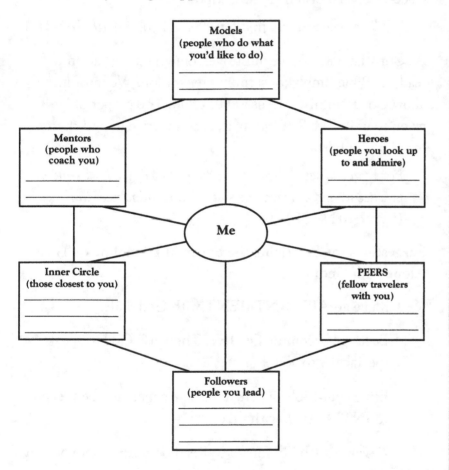

Your Heavenly Father

Although you are a leader, you do not cease being a child of God. The most common term used in the New Testament to describe God is not Creator, King, Ruler, or Savior. It is Father.

And you are first His son or daughter before you are a leader. He calls you to lead others, but only as you remain dependent upon Him. This will require conscious steps on your part.

God has established a Kingdom that requires us to receive His love before we are capable of loving the people He has given us to care for. We cannot be grace-givers unless we are first grace-receivers. Listen to the Scripture:

> *We love, because He first loved us.* (1 John 4:19 NASB)

As Christian leaders, we must overcome the temptation to read the Bible simply for sermon preparation. We must first allow God to minister to us as His child. The proper order is given to us in Ezra 7:10: study it, then practice it, and then teach it to others.

> *For Ezra had set his heart to study the law of the LORD and to practice it, and to teach His statutes and ordinances in Israel.* (Ezra 7:10 NASB)

Suggestions for Practicing the Spiritual Discipline of Time Alone with God:

- Make an **APPOINTMENT** with God daily.

- Begin by becoming **QUIET.** Then, ask God to speak specifically to you.

- Bring your Bible, a pen, and some paper, and be prepared to **INTERACT** with God.

- Develop a **PLAN** for study. Read Scripture that you can digest in one sitting.

- Determine to read until you receive a **PRINCIPLE** or truth to practice.

- **WRITE** out what God is saying through His Word:

  1) One Time: Describe what the passage said to the original audience.

  2) All Time: Identify a universal principle that is relevant for all time.

  3) Now Time: Record what you can do to apply this truth to your life.

- Learn to **MEDITATE** on the specific word God has for you.

- **PRAY** through the passage of Scripture asking God to build truth in you.

- Internalize the Word through **OBEDIENCE.**

KEY POINTS

Your Family

God designed families to be a refuge where we can experience intimacy and unconditional love. We are to know and be fully known without fear of rejection. Just as a scientist has a laboratory in which he can experiment, families are to be a safe place to practice listening, loving, forgiving, and resolving conflict. All of these prepare us for the unsafe world we enter each day.

In other words, our spiritual leadership and service begins in the home. We serve there first, and then we have credibility to serve outside the home. A good rule to follow is, if it doesn't work at home, don't export it. Listen to Scripture:

> *But if anyone does not provide for his own, and especially for those of his household, he has denied the faith and is worse than an unbeliever.* (1 Timothy 5:8 NASB)

Characteristics of Strong Families:

- They express **APPRECIATION** for each other on a regular basis.

- They structure their lives so they can spend **TIME** together.

- They deal with problems in a **POSITIVE** way.

- They demonstrate a strong **COMMITMENT** to each other.

- They continually **COMMUNICATE** with one another.

- They share the same **VALUE** system.

- The parents **MODEL** what it means to bless other members.

Finding a Paul

A "Paul" is a mentor. All leaders ought to have mentors, regardless of how successful they are. Everyone needs a mentor, including mentors. Mentors are people who have traveled further than we have in their leadership journey, and they can pass on what they have learned.

Counsel in the heart of man is like deep water, but a man of understanding will draw it out. (Prov. 20:5 NKJV)

We recommend you begin each year by writing down four or five areas in which you would like to grow. Then, instead of looking for one perfect mentor to meet all those needs, find a specialist for each one. Mentors are not impossible to find. They are everywhere. If you can't seem to find one, follow these steps:

- Pray that God will open your eyes to mentors you may not realize are nearby.

- Set a realistic standard. Don't expect a perfect mentor. Mentors are humans too.

- Look for strengths in a potential mentor that you want to develop in yourself.

- Be open to multiple mentors who could effectively invest in you.

- Recognize that mentors may be distant. Be willing to do it by phone or email.

What to Look for in a Mentor:

In addition to possessing a specific strength, be sure your mentor is:

Godly: They should demonstrate godly character worth imitating.

Objective: They must be able to see your strengths and weaknesses.

Authentic: They must be real. You can see their genuine, transparent heart.

Loyal: They must be loyal to relationships and be able to keep confidentiality.

Serving: They should be willing to give generously of their time and resources.

Finding a Barnabas

A "Barnabas" is a peer and a friend. They are accountability partners for us. They are important because they motivate us to keep our commitments to God and others. They ask us hard questions about our spiritual lives, our motives in ministry, our goals, our characters, and our relationships. Finding a Barnabas is like receiving a gift from God. They know us well, and they love us anyway. We don't need to hide anything from them. They motivate us to reach our potential. When you meet with your Barnabas, exchange a list of questions you wish to discuss. Some suggestions might be:

CHECK YOUR HEART

- Have you spent time with God on a daily basis?

- How have you been tempted this week?

- Do you have any unconfessed sin in your life? How is your thought life?

- Are your priorities in the right order? Are you reaching your goals?

- Have you been completely honest with me in your answers to these questions?

What to Look for in an Accountability Partner:

Ask accountability partners to make a pact with you. Look for these qualities in them:

Probing: They ask probing questions to help you see needs in your life.

Authentic: They are honest and genuine about their own weaknesses.

Challenging: They help you press on to a new level of leadership and obedience.

Trustworthy: They value honesty and can handle anything you share with them.

> *And let us consider how to stimulate one another to love and good deeds, not forsaking our own assembling together, as is the*

habit of some, but encouraging one another; and all the more as you see the day drawing near. (Heb. 10:24–25 NASB)

A man of too many friends comes to ruin, but there is a friend who sticks closer than a brother. (Prov. 18:24 NASB)

Finding a Timothy

The Bible is clear that leaders are to select and train people for a life of ministry. Jesus selected and trained twelve. Paul found young men like Titus and Timothy. A "Timothy" is someone who is following you in his or her leadership journey but is eager to grow as a leader. Every leader ought to find apprentices who learn as they serve alongside the leader. In fact, when they learn, they are also called to pass on what they receive.

The things which you have heard from me in the presence of many witnesses, entrust these to faithful men who will be able to teach others also. (2 Tim. 2:2 NASB)

Leaders should never do ministry alone. They should always be training others as they do the work God has called them to do. A leader's ministry may add to the Kingdom, but when they train a disciple, they multiply for the Kingdom.

What to Look for in a Mentee:

The qualities to look for as you select people to mentor or disciple are these:

Faithful: They are faithful to commitments they have already made.

Available: They have the time to commit to learning from you.

Courageous Leadership Workbook

Initiative: They show initiative in their obedience to God and desire to serve.

Teachable: They are willing to learn from you.

Hungry: They have a passion and eagerness to grow as a leader.

Alarm Bells for Leaders

The goal of this network is to help you become a leader of integrity. We need God and people to send us signals when we are failing to live or lead effectively. Often, public buildings have alarm bells that send a signal when something is wrong. The following are questions that should ring as alarm bells for leaders:

Is my personal walk with GOD up to date?

Are you hearing from God daily? Can others sense you've been in His presence?

Am I keeping my PRIORITIES straight?

Are you living out what you say is most important to you? Do you schedule priorities?

Am I asking myself the hard QUESTIONS?

Why do you do what you do (motives)? How do you pursue your goals (presumption)?

Am I ACCOUNTABLE to someone in authority?

Who is your God-given leader to whom you are accountable?

Am I listening to what God is saying to the WHOLE body of Christ?

Do you have a narrow view of God based on your own little world?

Am I over-concerned with building my IMAGE?

Are you preoccupied with how you look and what others think about you?

Am I overly impressed by either CRITICISM or FLATTERY?

Do you believe everything people say? Are you swayed too much by human opinion?

Am I a "LONER" in my ministry?

Do you tend to be independent, or have you built a network or community around you?

Am I aware of my WEAKNESSES?

Have you recognized your weaknesses? Do you address them or ignore them?

Is my CALLING constantly before me?

Does your divine calling give you passion each week to serve God?

Courageous Leadership Workbook

ASSESSMENT: *How do you give God priority in your daily network?*

_____

_____

_____

_____

_____

Review the diagram for "Your Network" on page 27. In which areas do you need to find people with whom you can build key relationships?

_____

_____

_____

_____

_____

ACTION PLAN

APPLICATION: *Identify one person with whom you can be totally honest. This person should be someone with whom you can share your deepest struggles and even discuss your motives. Ask them to meet with you regularly and hold you accountable for your commitments. Who will this be?*

Write down when you will meet to ask them to be part of your network.

Christ, the Great Communicator

Lesson 3

Improving Your Communication Skills by Imitating the Master

Death and life are in the power of the tongue,
and those who love it will eat its fruit.
(Prov. 18:21 NASB)

BIBLICAL BASIS

The success of your leadership, your marriage, and your relationships with others depends a great deal on your ability to communicate. Many of the best thinkers are not leaders. Why? They cannot communicate. Your leadership rests on your ability to connect with people, share your ideas and vision, and motivate them to partner with you. One former world leader said, "If I could start all over again, I would go back to school and learn to communicate."

Matthew 13

Jesus is the greatest communicator who ever walked the earth. In John 1, He is called "the Word." In Matthew 13 we see an example of His effective style. Christ, the Great Communicator, teaches us how to relate truth to our people today.

1. SIMPLIFY THE MESSAGE
(Matt. 13:3, 10–13)

Our lesson: It's not just what you say, but *how* you say it.

Jesus shared most of His message through stories. He shared seven of them in this chapter alone. He used the power of simple, familiar narratives. The educator takes something simple and makes it complicated. The communicator takes something complicated and makes it simple. Jesus gave His listeners a point for their minds and a picture for their hearts.

Jesus' rules of communication:

a. Strong beginnings   d. Familiar pictures

b. One theme   e. Clear objectives

c. Simple language   f. Heart responses

2. KNOW THE PEOPLE
(Matt. 13:1–2, 9)

Our lesson: It's not just what you say, but how they *hear* it.

Jesus saw the people and perceived their needs. It is difficult to effectively communicate with an audience without knowing something about them. Most learning takes place in the arena of a person's familiarity or interest. Jesus identified with people. To become more like Him we'll have to become more "people-oriented" and less "lesson-oriented." Public speakers teach lessons; communicators teach people.

Public Speaker	Communicator
• Puts the message before the people	• Puts the people before the message
• Asks: "What do I have?"	• Asks: "What do they need?"
• The key is techniques	• The key is atmosphere
• Content-oriented	• Change-oriented
• Goal is to complete the message	• Goal is to complete the people

Jesus used what was cultural to say what is timeless. He connected with His listeners where they were in order to lead them where they needed to be. Paul did the same thing in Acts 17 when he spoke at Mars Hill. So did Peter when he spoke at Pentecost in Acts 2. These men all communicated truth but did so from the perspective of their listeners.

3. SEIZE THE MOMENT (Matt. 13:2, 14–17, 57–58)

Our lesson: It's not just what you say, but *when* you say it.

At times, Jesus was conspicuously silent when it was tempting to speak out. At other times, He spoke when it was in His selfish interest to stay quiet. He understood timing. The Scripture says when the people came, Jesus spoke (v. 2). The Scripture also says when the people rejected the message, He did not perform any more miracles (v. 57–58). Effective leaders know when to relay a message for best results. God is a master at timing. Galatians 4:4 (NASB) says, "When the fullness of the time came, God sent forth His Son."

Questions to ask about timing:

- Who is my audience?

- What are their questions and needs right now?

- What needs to be accomplished most?

- What is God's answer to their questions and needs?

- Are they ready to receive it?

- How can I build a bridge of relationship that will bear the weight of truth?

EXAMINE THE WORD

4. SHOW THE TRUTH (Matt. 13:54)

Our lesson: It's not just what you say, but how you *show* it.

He came to His hometown and began teaching them in their synagogue, so that they were astonished, and said, "Where did this man get this wisdom and these miraculous powers?" (Matt. 13:54 NASB)

Jesus' credibility came not only from His words, but also from His life. He modeled His teaching. It was show and tell. He said "follow Me," not just "listen to Me" (Matt. 4:19).

Every time you speak, your audience is quietly asking:

- Why should I listen to you?

- Can I trust you?

- Do you care for me?

- Do you know your subject?

Author Charles Allen describes Jesus this way:

> He might have preached lengthy sermons on the dignity of labor, temptation, how to enjoy life, the immortality of the soul, the worth of children, and the fact that God answers prayer. Instead, He worked in a carpenter's shop; He met and conquered temptation in the wilderness; He went to parties and laughed with other happy people; He raised the dead; He stopped to love little children; and after He prayed, the power of the Lord was present.
>
> He might have talked long and loud about the need of man for human sympathy, the worth of womanhood, the blessing of humility, and the equal worth of all men. Instead, He wept at the grave of a friend, He treated all women with deep respect, He took a towel and washed His disciples' feet, He gave His time to the poor and outcasts.
>
> Instead of talking about how He could transform lives, He took a harlot and made her the first herald of the resurrection. Instead of preaching that people need bread, He fed the multitude. Instead of arguing the spirit is stronger than matter, He walked on water. Instead of telling people how bad it is to be crippled, He said, "Arise, take up your bed and walk." Instead of merely telling people they should forgive, while He was dying and being spit on He prayed, "Father, forgive them."

5. SHARE THE PASSION
(Matt. 13:53–57)

Our lesson: It's not just what you say, but *why* you say it.

Jesus spoke from His convictions. His convictions enabled Him to conclude that a prophet is not without honor except in his own country (v. 57). His words were from His heart. He spoke with passion and demonstrated obedience to

43

His heavenly Father. He had nothing to prove, nothing to lose, and nothing to hide. He didn't speak out of routine or obligation. When He spoke, His words always had great meaning.

There are no boring subjects, only boring speakers. There are no small audiences, only small speakers. If you are interested in your audience, they will be interested in you.

Tips on speaking with passion:

- Speak on themes that you own for yourself.

- Be impact-conscious rather than image-conscious.

- Be authentic. Lock onto a pair of eyes with each point.

- Paint pictures in your listeners' hearts.

- Know what your goal is when you speak.

- Prepare with prayer and let God build a fire inside you.

6. SEEK THE RESPONSE (Matt. 13:51)

Our lesson: It's not just what you say, but how they *respond* to it.

After Jesus taught, He asked, "Have you understood these things?" He was probing to make sure His listeners could apply the truth. Jesus always spoke with a goal in mind. There was something for the audience to know, something for them to feel, and something for them to do. A good message always includes all three of these ingredients. This will require us to research our audience, not just our message.

The fact is: 20 percent of most audiences will act on their own

80 percent of most audiences will not act on their own

Tips on helping people to respond to truth:

- Have a clear objective for your listener to act on.

- Reduce it to a simple phrase and write it down.

- Use a "hook" the listener can grasp and remember.

- Give them a point for their head and a picture for their heart.

- Provide a vehicle for them to use in response.

- Ask for what you want them to do.

You must:

- Believe in your God.

- Believe in your message.

- Believe in yourself.

- Believe in your audience.

KEY POINTS

Question: What is it you desire your listeners to do when you speak to them?

_____

_____

Question: How can you best encourage them to take that step of obedience?

_____

_____

_____

Steps to Reduce Your Anxiety as a Communicator

ACTION PLAN

1. Prepare extensively. (The more ready you are, the more relaxed you'll be.)

2. Memorize your first burst. (Know your first three sentences or opening story.)

3. Speak to friendly eyes. (To get comfortable, focus on faces that are interested.)

4. Dress comfortably for the audience. (If you don't, you may get preoccupied.)

5. Take deep breaths before you begin. (This keeps you from nervously rushing.)

6. Visualize yourself being effective. (See God using you to impact your audience.)

7. State your goal to yourself before you begin. (Be clear on what your target is.)

8. Use visual aids. (This can make the message memorable and keep the attention off of you.)

9. Come to the meeting room early. (Arrive fifteen minutes early to remove surprises.)

10. Pray, pray, pray! (Lean on God to communicate His vision through you.)

    Be anxious for nothing, but in everything by prayer and supplication with thanksgiving let your requests be made known to God. And the peace of God, which surpasses all comprehension, will guard your hearts and your minds in Christ Jesus. (Phil. 4:6–7 NASB)

ASSESSMENT: *Jesus demonstrated six principles of communication. Which of these six do you already effectively practice? On which do you need to improve?*

_____

_____

_____

_____

_____

_____

_____

Courageous Leadership Workbook

APPLICATION: *What action will you take to become a better communicator? How will you communicate differently this week when you speak to people?*

_____

_____

_____

_____

_____

_____

_____

_____

_____

_____

The words of the wise are like goads, and the words of scholars are like well-driven nails, given by one Shepherd. (Ecc. 12:11 NKJV)

Leading When Times Are Tough

Lesson 4

Handling Difficult People and Situations

You have heard that it was said, "You shall love your neighbor and hate your enemy." But I say to you, love your enemies and pray for those who persecute you, so that you may be sons of your Father who is in heaven . . . For if you love those who love you, what reward do you have? Do not even the tax collectors do the same? If you greet only your brothers, what more are you doing than others? Do not even the Gentiles do the same? Therefore you are to be perfect, as your heavenly Father is perfect. (Matt. 5:43–48 NASB)

No doubt you will experience some difficult and draining moments as you attempt to lead others. Leadership can be a thankless, lonely, and even discouraging task, simply because you are the target for the criticism. It's very likely you will feel both *affirmed* and *attacked* as you lead.

You must remember that both you and your people remain "human" even though you are Christians. This means you'll face conflict before the journey is finished. People possess different perspectives, personalities, and struggles that cause them to react the way they do. Thank God for His grace. It has been said that the church is a lot like Noah's ark. The stench on the inside would be intolerable if it weren't for the storm on the outside! Let's examine how to deal with difficult people effectively.

Discussion:

Take a moment to discuss some of the difficult situations you have faced in the past as a leader. Do you see any patterns?

Often, the most common sources of conflict and difficulty with people are as follows:

- Personality and relationship clashes

- Unspoken and unmet expectations

- Insecurity and identity issues

- Unresolved conflict from past wounds

- Independent attitudes and inflexible perspectives

Foundational Principles Leaders Must Understand

KEY POINTS

- In relationships, leaders often must practice the 101 Percent Principle: find the **1 percent** you can agree with and give it 100 percent of your attention.

- In relationships, it is better to build a **FENCE** at the top of the cliff, than a hospital at the bottom. (Take steps to prevent potential trouble.)

- When the **EMOTION** expressed far outweighs the issue at hand, there is a hidden issue to face.

- When a person's **EMOTIONAL** needs outweigh their intelligence, they won't be logical.

- Hurting people naturally **HURT** people.

- As leaders, we must never place our **EMOTIONAL** health in the hands of someone else.

- It is possible for a leader to sabotage himself. He might win an argument, but ultimately he **LOSES** more than he gains.

- We must practice the Law of Connection: leaders touch a **HEART** before they ask for a hand.

Remember . . .

- Conflict is **Normal.** *(It is going to happen because we are different.)*

- Conflict is **Neutral.** *(It is neither destructive nor constructive in itself.)*

- Conflict is **Natural.** *(It is universal; you're not alone in your humanity.)*

Five Options When Faced with Conflict

1. I'll get **THEM!** (retaliation)

2. I'll get **OUT!** (escape and avoidance)

3. I'll give **IN!** (surrender)

4. I'll go **HALF!** (compromise)

5. I'll **DEAL** with it! (address the issue)

KEY POINTS

Handling Criticism in a Healthy Way

- Understand the difference between constructive and destructive criticism.

- Take God seriously, but don't take yourself too seriously. Laugh at yourself.

- Look beyond the criticism and see the critic. What's behind their criticism?

- Recognize that good people get criticized. Even Jesus was criticized!

- Keep physically and spiritually in shape. Stay strong for such attacks.

- Don't just see the critic; see the crowd. Don't let one person bring you down.

- Wait for time to demonstrate what is right. Allow God to bring things to light.

- Concentrate on your mission. Change your mistakes, not your mission.

Five Stages: How Paul Faced Conflict

The Apostle Paul faced conflict with a man named Philemon. He foresaw the fact that they didn't share the same perspective on Onesimus, a runaway slave belonging to Philemon. The following steps are the Apostle Paul's course on conflict management. He communicates masterfully with Philemon in his letter and gives five stages to walk through in the process:

1. COMPLIMENT STAGE (v. 4–7)

Just as Paul began by affirming Philemon, we must begin by focusing on positive qualities. Practice the 101 Percent Principle mentioned previously. Always open by focusing on the positive and what you have in common.

2. COMPROMISE STAGE (v. 8–13)

Paul chose to compromise and appeal to Philemon rather than make demands. We must be willing to assume some responsibility for the conflict, if possible. As you bring up the issue in conflict, recognize the differences in motivation and temperament; meet halfway.

3. CHOICE STAGE (v. 14)

Next, Paul communicates the decision in front of Philemon. In the same way, you must lay out the choice in front of both parties, as you understand it. Maintain their dignity, if possible. Take steps to sustain friendship.

4. CHALLENGE STAGE (v. 15–20)

Paul then challenged Philemon to do what was right. You must commit yourself to the steps you will take, then extend a clear challenge and await a response. Settle the issue, if possible. Lay out good boundaries and parameters to keep the relationship healthy. Don't let enemies accumulate.

5. CONFIDENCE STAGE (v. 21–22)

Finally, Paul closed by expressing confidence that Philemon would take the high road. End by expressing sincere confidence in your adversary as a person. Let him know you trust him to do what's right and nothing will prevent you from loving him. Remember, it is more important to win a "soul" than to win an argument.

Biblical Confrontation

When someone under your care has clearly done wrong, the Bible calls us to confront them on issues regarding sin, failure to keep a public commitment, a destructive attitude, harmful conversation, etc. If you waver on whether the Bible addresses this subject, review the following passages:

EXAMINE THE WORD

- *Colossians 3:16*—We are to admonish one another with wisdom.

- *1 Thessalonians 5:14*—We are to remind, warn, and admonish the fainthearted.

- *2 Timothy 4:2–4*—We must preach, reprove, rebuke, and exhort with patience.

- *Colossians 1:28*—We must admonish (warn by reminding) people.

- *Titus 1:13*—We are instructed to reprove that others may be sound in faith.

Remember, your goal is to see people transformed by the power of God. Your objective is not condemnation but restoration. People must know we love them, but we love truth more than anything else in the world. An unexamined life is not worth living.

Steps Toward Effective Confrontation

1. **Pray through your own anger.**
   Don't let emotion lead you. Wait until you're objective, but deal with issues before they become too big.

2. **You initiate the contact.**
   Don't wait for them to initiate. Scripture beckons you to make things right whether you are the offender or the offended person.

3. **Begin with affirmation.**
   Speak words of love and encouragement first. Then, receive fresh permission to challenge them, and to be honest about what you see.

4. **Tell them that you have a problem or a struggle.**
   Don't say it's their problem but yours; own the fact that you have wrestled through dealing with the issue.

5. **Bring up the issue, and explain you don't understand what's happened.**
   The meeting may be more of a "clarification" than a confrontation. Give them the benefit of the doubt and allow them to explain themselves. Aim to clarify.

6. **Listen and allow them to respond.**
   At this point, you must stop to let them respond. They may present a new perspective that will help you both.

CHECK YOUR HEART

7. **Establish forgiveness and repentance, if necessary.**
   Connect the issue you are correcting with who they are in Christ. Don't conclude the meeting until forgiveness is extended and issues are clear and resolved.

8. Compromise on opinions, but not on biblical convictions or principles.

Determine where you must take a stand. Be flexible with your own opinions or preferences, but not on issues where the Bible has clearly spoken.

9. Pray and affirm your love as you close your time together.

Always close these times with prayer. Give your opponents hope and remind them of their places in God's heart and yours; help them to never question that they are loved.

Pass the Blessing, Please!

While confronting conflict is important, it may be only a symptom of the real issue. The real issue is always an issue of the heart. Often, the primary reason people experience unresolved conflict and difficulties is that they are hungry for "the blessing." In the Old Testament, men would give a "blessing" to their children; rabbis would "bless" their students, and craftsmen would "bless" their apprentices. The "blessing" consists of these elements:

- **MEANINGFUL TOUCH:** Patriarchs laid their hands on their shoulders or embraced them.

- **AFFIRMING WORDS:** Patriarchs spoke words of encouragement to them.

- **THE EXPRESSION OF HIGH VALUE:** Patriarchs shared the value they added to others.

- **THE DESCRIPTION OF A SPECIAL FUTURE:** Patriarchs used word pictures to share their potential.

- **GENUINE COMMITMENT:** Patriarchs committed themselves to see it come to pass.

Often we cannot put words to it, but we are like Jacob as we wrestle all our lives to get the "blessing." We seek the approval of those in authority, from our parents to our supervisors on the job. As fallen people, we have lost our security and sense of significance. In a very real sense, this may explain why so many seem to have lost their sense of identity. Hence, we tend to struggle to meet personal needs in an unhealthy way.

Components for Inward Health

1. A sense of **WORTH.**
   If this is missing, we feel inferior.

2. A sense of **BELONGING.**
   If this is missing, we feel insecure.

3. A sense of **COMPETENCE.**
   If this is missing, we feel inadequate.

4. A sense of **PURPOSE.**
   If this is missing, we feel insignificant.

Courageous Leadership Workbook

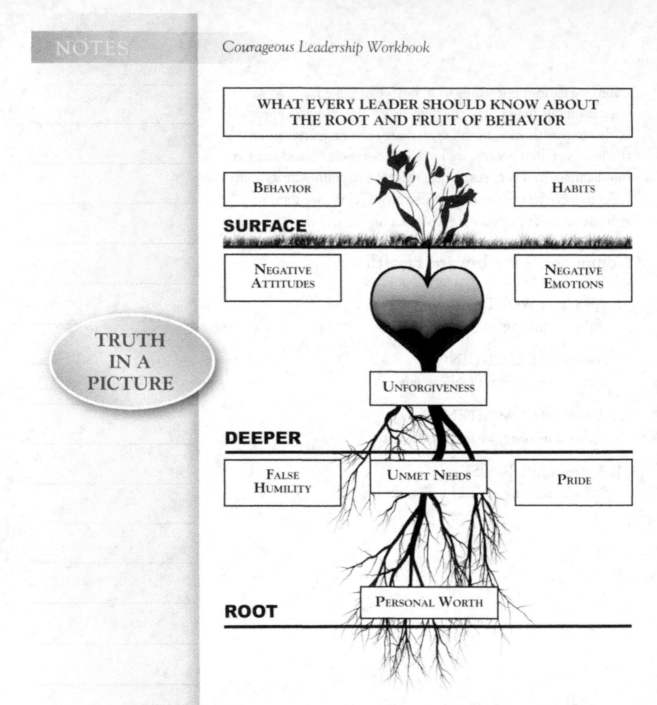

WHAT EVERY LEADER SHOULD KNOW ABOUT THE ROOT AND FRUIT OF BEHAVIOR

BEHAVIOR

HABITS

SURFACE

NEGATIVE ATTITUDES

NEGATIVE EMOTIONS

TRUTH IN A PICTURE

UNFORGIVENESS

DEEPER

FALSE HUMILITY

UNMET NEEDS

PRIDE

PERSONAL WORTH

ROOT

What we can see above the surface are behaviors and habits. Someone may become a source of conflict or hurt because something isn't right in his life. You don't have to dig very far in a conversation with him to spot negative attitudes and emotions, like anger or depression. If you probe a bit further,

60

you will often begin to see unforgiveness. Generally speaking, people have negative emotions when they have not been able to forgive someone or let go of something from their pasts. If you dig deeper, you uncover unmet needs. Obviously, the negative person expected someone to meet a need. When that person failed to do so, the negative person refuses to forgive him.

Ultimately, however, at the root of this issue is self-worth. The person does not believe he has value, and he seeks unhealthy ways to make up for it. He may spark conflict, seek attention, become depressed, hostile, driven, independent, oversensitive, fearful, ungrateful, or inexpressive because he feels unworthy.

This is why giving the blessing is so important. Because so many families don't know how to do this today, the family of God must step in and do it instead. You represent a leader in the family of God. You must bless and teach others to bless people. This means you must be discerning. There will be times you must confront a person who has become a source of conflict. However, there will be times you must offer the blessing to those who are in need of it. If you create an environment that blesses those in need, you will likely prevent conflict in the long run.

ASSESSMENT: *Evaluate your ministry. How much conflict do you experience? Is it a place where the blessing is offered?*

ACTION PLAN

_____

_____

_____

_____

61

APPLICATION: *Identify one person who is a source of conflict for you as a leader. Diagnose his need. Does he need to be confronted or does he need a blessing? Go give him what he needs.*

_____

_____

_____

_____

The Five Levels of Leadership

Lesson 5

A Look at Why People Follow Their Leaders

Then He appointed twelve, that they might be with Him and that He might send them out to preach.
(Mark 3:14 NKJV)

People follow leaders for a variety of reasons. As leaders increase their influence with people, they expand the reasons for others to follow them. The leader's effectiveness must increase with time if he is going to attract new people as well as retain present followers. The goal of this lesson is to help you understand what level you're on with your people and understand how to deepen your influence.

The diagram that follows describes five levels of leadership. The level of influence you have as a leader is directly related to the relationship you have with your people. As you climb from one level of leadership to the next, your effectiveness will increasingly grow.

NOTES

PERSONHOOD

RESPECT: People follow because of who you are and what you represent.

NOTE: This step is reserved for leaders who have spent years growing people and organizations. Few make it to this level.

PEOPLE DEVELOPMENT

REPRODUCTION: People follow because of what you have done for them.

NOTE: This is where long-range growth occurs. Your commitment to developing leaders will insure ongoing growth to the church and to individuals.

PRODUCTION

RESULTS: People follow because of what you have done for the organization or church.

NOTE: This is where success is sensed by most people. They like you and what you are doing. Problems are fixed with little effort because of momentum. People sense godly success for the church.

PERMISSION

RELATIONSHIPS: People follow because they want to.

NOTE: People will follow you beyond your stated authority. This level allows work and ministry to be fun and joyful.

CAUTION: If you stay too long on this level without rising, you will cause highly motivated people to become restless.

POSITION

RIGHTS: People follow you because they have to.

NOTE: Your influence on this level will not extend beyond the lines of your job description. The only authority you have is what your title gives you. The longer you stay at this level, the higher the turnover rate and the lower the morale of the people.

Five Levels of Leadership

1. POSITION

People follow you because they **HAVE** to.

This is the lowest level of influence for a leader. Leaders must rely on their title to get people to follow them. There is nothing wrong with titles, but if you must have a title for people to follow you, something is wrong. Jesus never had a position or title, and yet He had huge influence through building relationships, meeting needs, and offering hope. His authority came from God and the life He lived, not from an assigned position or title. At level one, authority comes only from your title.

Biblical Example: **REHOBOAM**

"If you will be a servant to this people today . . . then they will be your servants forever." But he forsook the counsel of the elders . . . (1 Kings 12:7–8 NASB)

BIBLICAL BASIS

When Solomon died, Rehoboam took over as king of Israel. He got power hungry and acted foolishly. Rehoboam listened to the counsel of his peers rather than the elders, and instead of lightening their load, he increased their labor. The people followed him only because he was the king; there was no relationship. Ultimately, Rehoboam was responsible for dividing the nation into two kingdoms, the Northern and the Southern. He never moved past leading from mere title and position.

The Law of the Lid: leadership ability determines a person's level of effectiveness.

2. PERMISSION

People follow you because they **WANT** to.

Influence at this level extends beyond your stated authority because you have connected with people relationally. You have communicated trust and credibility, and they now choose to follow you out of devotion rather than duty. This level is an improvement from level one because you are influencing from your person, not your position. However, leaders must recognize there is a difference between being liked as a friend and being followed as a leader. Experiencing a mere relationship without producing any results for the church or organization will eventually fail to motivate people to make sacrifices, take risks, and follow you.

Biblical Example: **NEHEMIAH**

"You see the distress that we are in, how Jerusalem lies waste, and its gates are burned with fire. Come and let us build the wall of Jerusalem, that we may no longer be a reproach." . . . So they said, "Let us rise up and build." Then they set their hands to this good work. . . . So I answered them, and said to them, "The God of heaven Himself will prosper us." (Neh. 2:17–18, 20 NKJV)

Nehemiah challenged the people to face the reality that the broken walls of Jerusalem were not only an embarrassment to their nation but, more importantly, to God. With a hammer in one hand and a weapon in the other, the people moved to action because Nehemiah connected with them on many levels relationally. Reflect on what he did:

- Challenged their national pride
- Motivated them to have ownership
- Enlarged their vision spiritually
- Mobilized them to action
- Identified God's presence
- Set the goal
- Encouraged their participation
- Divided the responsibilities

The Law of Connection: leaders touch a heart before they ask for a hand.

3. PRODUCTION

People will follow you because of what you've **DONE** for the organization or church.

They like the results they've seen. At this level, they not only enjoy a relationship with the leader, but they enjoy the results he or she has produced. There is fruit in the church and fulfillment in the people who participated in the journey. People love to follow a leader who gets things done. They love to be part of a team that wins. This describes leadership at this level.

Biblical Example: **DAVID**

Then all the tribes of Israel came to David at Hebron and spoke, saying, "Indeed we are your bone and your flesh. Also, in time past, when Saul was king over us, you were the one who led Israel out and brought them in; and the LORD said to you, 'You shall shepherd My people Israel, and be ruler over Israel.'" (2 Sam. 5:1–2 NKJV)

EXAMINE THE WORD

David was called a man after God's own heart. His passion for God was first exposed when he fought Goliath as a young teenager. As David matured, he gained respect as the nation saw his responses to Saul's repeated attempts to kill him. By the time he reigned as king over Israel, David had progressed well beyond the first two levels of leadership. In fact, David led even before he had a title. He had built relationships with key people. He had proven himself in battle. He had learned team-building skills, he made decisions intuitively, and his vision energized the people. The result was strategic military victories. With each conquest, David gained more influence and respect. David followed these principles:

KEY POINTS

- Good leaders offer a clear vision that unites the people.

- Good leaders put God's agenda first and seek to please Him.

- Good leaders solve problems and produce results.

- Good leaders build teams who share responsibility and credit.

The Law of Respect: people naturally follow a leader stronger than themselves.

4. PEOPLE DEVELOPMENT

People will follow you because of what you've done for **THEM.**

At this level, a leader gains a new level of authority. He has personally impacted the lives of his team members. The leader has poured his life into others. He has not only been a minister, but a mentor to others. He has developed the potential of key people. On this level, a leader reproduces his life. Multiplication occurs.

Biblical Example: **PAUL**

And the things that you have heard from me among many witnesses, commit these to faithful men who will be able to teach others also. (2 Tim. 2:2 NKJV)

Paul referred to Timothy as "a true son in the faith" (1 Tim. 1:2). Timothy was feeling inadequate for the task of pastoring the church in Ephesus. Paul mentored him face to face as well as through letters to encourage him as an emerging leader. Titus was another leader in whom Paul saw potential. He gave Titus tough church assignments to stretch him. Priscilla and Aquila were also mentored by Paul as they launched a church in Asia. Others were Luke, Silas, Onesimus, and Philemon.

Paul multiplied the church because he led leaders, not merely followers. He operated at level four with many people.

But it didn't stop there. Paul exhorted his young disciples to be leaders who multiplied. Let's look at Paul's strategy to promote explosive growth:

1. Attract and select sharp potential leaders

2. Mentor and develop them as emerging leaders

3. Give them assignments to prove their potential

4. Release them to serve and reproduce other leaders

The Law of Explosive Growth: to add growth, lead followers; to multiply, lead leaders.

5. PERSONHOOD

People will follow you because of **WHO YOU ARE,** what you represent.

Leaders at this level have spent years growing people and organizations.

Biblical Example: **SAMUEL**

So Samuel grew, and the LORD was with him and let none of his words fall to the ground. And all Israel from Dan to Beersheba knew that Samuel had been established as a prophet of the LORD. (1 Sam. 3:19–20 NKJV)

EXAMINE THE WORD

As a young child Samuel learned to recognize the voice of God. His first prophecy was against the family of his mentor, Eli. He had the courage to speak the truth in love. That was the first of many times God would use Samuel to speak a hard truth while leading God's people. Samuel identified with the Israelites, and they respected his faithful walk with God. They listened to his counsel, whether it was for a strategy to use against the Philistines or direction for their future. Samuel gained so much influence within the nation of Israel, he had the authority to depose Saul as king and anoint David as his replacement. Samuel exhibited the heart of a servant leader. The impact of Samuel's life was so great that when he died, all of Israel gathered to mourn his loss (1 Sam. 25:1).

At this final step on the ladder to leadership, Samuel demonstrated these qualities:

- A faithful servant of the Lord

- An example of a life lived with integrity

- A consistent producer of leaders over the years

Moses' Steps to Leadership

Moses' leadership journey is summarized in Hebrews 11:24–29. His life of leadership encompassed all five levels:

1. Position

EXAMINE
THE
WORD

Moses grew up in Pharaoh's palace as a prince of Egypt (Ex. 2:10). He had the finest education, knew the "who's who" of Egypt, and basically had access to all that the world had to offer.

2. Permission

Moses felt compelled to help his fellow Hebrews long before God met him at the burning bush. Even though he grew up in the Egyptian culture, he identified with his true heritage. Moses chose "to suffer affliction with the people of God, [rather] than to enjoy the pleasures of sin for a season" (Heb. 11:25 KJV).

3. Production

The pendulum in Moses' life of faith swung from one extreme to another. In Exodus 3–4 he gave God multiple excuses, "I am slow of speech . . . please send someone else." In Exodus 7–11 he freed Israel from their bondage in Egypt. With each plague, the people saw God's hand of deliverance, and they became willing to follow Moses anywhere.

4. People Development

Moses delegated authority and equipped seventy elders, following his father-in-law's advice (Ex. 18). His life-long mentoring relationship with Joshua gave him a successor who would lead the Israelites into the Promised Land (Num. 27:20–23).

5. Personhood

Moses was an undisputed leader when it came to endurance. No other leader in Scripture endured the wilderness with two million people. In the midst of their whining and complaining, Moses repeatedly interceded on their behalf. He often reminded God that in spite of their disobedience, they were His chosen people (Ex. 32:1–35).

And the children of Israel wept for Moses in the plains of Moab thirty days. (Deut. 34:8a KJV)

Climbing the Steps of Leadership

The following truths will enable you to interpret the "Five Levels of Leadership" diagram.

KEY POINTS

• The higher you go, **THE LONGER IT TAKES.**

- The higher you go, **THE HIGHER YOUR LEVEL OF COMMITMENT.**

- The higher you go, **THE EASIER IT IS TO LEAD.**

- The higher you go, **THE GREATER THE GROWTH.**

- You never leave the **BASE LEVEL,** or the levels below where you are.

- As a leader, you won't be on the same **LEVEL** with all of your people.

- You must work to carry other **LEADERS** with you up the steps.

How Do We Climb the Leadership Steps?

- Consistently ask God to **BUILD** you into a more **EFFECTIVE** leader.

- Develop confidence in your **PEOPLE SKILLS.**

- See every relationship you have as a chance to **DEVELOP** that person.

- Walk slowly through the **CROWDS.**

- Constantly keep a list of potential **LEADERS** in whom you can invest.

- Prioritize discipleship: find systematic ways to **TRAIN** people.

- Select and **MENTOR** key leaders.

- Live a model life that others would want to **IMITATE.**

- Recognize that **PEOPLE** are your most valuable asset.

ASSESSMENT: *As you consider these principles, think about what level you are on with the people you lead. List what it will take to move to the next level.*

ACTION PLAN

_____

_____

_____

_____

_____

APPLICATION: *What do you struggle with most in climbing the leadership steps? How can you begin to implement these steps?*

_____

_____

_____

_____

_____

The Art of the Basin and the Towel

Lesson 6
Developing the Qualities of a Servant Leader

BIBLICAL BASIS

But Jesus called them to Himself and said, "You know that the rulers of the Gentiles lord it over them, and their great men exercise authority over them. It is not this way among you, but whoever wishes to become great among you shall be your servant."
(Matt. 20:25–26 NASB)

The issue of servant-leadership is the single greatest contrast between spiritual and secular leadership. During His three-and-a-half year ministry, Jesus consistently taught His disciples that leadership means servanthood—as opposed to the "top down" attitude the Gentiles demonstrated during that time (Matt. 20:25).

In his book *In the Name of Jesus*, Henri Nouwen mentions three very real, yet subtle, temptations that any servant of Christ faces. They correspond with the three temptations our Lord faced before He began His earthly ministry (Matt. 4).

First Temptation: TO BE SELF-SUFFICIENT (SELF-RELIANT)

Satan told Jesus that if He was the Son of God, He should turn stones into bread. He should take charge. He should be self-reliant. This attitude stands in opposition to everything we know about the Kingdom. As leaders, we must foster our dependence on the Lord. Instead of being self-assured, we need to be open and vulnerable.

Second Temptation: TO BE SPECTACULAR (CELEBRITY MENTALITY)

Satan next tempted Jesus to throw Himself down and let God protect Him with His angels, to put on a show. Paul says this is to be deliberately renounced, as Jesus renounced it. In Nouwen's words, "Jesus refused to be a stunt man . . . He did not come to impress anyone." The goal of leadership is not to become a celebrity or to maintain an image, but to obey God.

Third Temptation: TO BE POWERFUL (IN CHARGE)

Satan's final temptation was for Jesus to bow down and worship him. If He would, Satan said he'd give Him all the kingdoms of this world. The temptation was to gain power now. After all, Jesus would eventually inherit all the kingdoms from His Father in heaven. Paul said: "We do not preach ourselves but Christ Jesus as Lord, and ourselves as your bondservants for Jesus' sake" (2 Cor. 4:5 NASB). Paul came to the Corinthians in weakness, not in strength, that their faith should not rest in the power of men but in the power of God. To lead is appropriate and necessary. But to push, manipulate, and control is never right. Put simply, one God is sufficient!

Horizontal Thinking vs. Vertical Thinking

On a regular basis, Jesus guided His disciples away from "horizontal thinking" and steered them toward "vertical thinking." Too often, they started looking at each other, comparing what they had done with what others had done. Often they worried if they were receiving enough credit or getting enough prestige. Even at the Last Supper . . .

> *Within minutes they were bickering over who of them would end up the greatest. But Jesus intervened: "Kings like to throw their weight around and people in authority like to give themselves fancy titles. It's not going to be that way with you. Let the senior among you become like the junior; let the leader act the part of the servant." (Luke 22:24–26 MSG)*

Practicing the Art of the Basin and Towel: John 13:1–20

In John 13, Jesus demonstrated servant leadership in a most vivid fashion: He washed the disciples' feet. Let's examine the text and see Christ's model as a servant leader.

Christ-like Servant Leaders . . .

1. Are motivated by LOVE to serve others. (John 13:1 MSG)

> *Just before the Passover Feast, Jesus knew that the time had come to leave this world to go to the Father. Having loved his dear companions, he continued to love them right to the end.*

Jesus' Love Was:

- **POSSESSIVE** (He loved His own)

- **CONTINUOUS** (He continued to love them to the end)

- **UNCONDITIONAL** (He even washed Judas's feet)

- **UNSELFISH** (He was serving in His most difficult hour)

"Everybody can be great . . . because everybody can serve. You don't have to have a college degree to serve. You don't have to make your subject and verb agree to serve. You only need a heart full of grace, a soul generated by love." —Dr. Martin Luther King Jr.

Question: Does love for people motivate you to lead? What is your primary motivation?

2. Possess a SECURITY that allows them to minister to others. (John 13:3 MSG)

Jesus knew that the Father had put him in complete charge of everything, that he came from God and was on his way back to God.

Jesus knew:

- His **POSITION** and was willing not to flaunt it.

- His **CALLING** and was willing to be faithful to it.

- His **FUTURE** and was willing to submit to it.

Jesus demonstrated He could serve others because He was secure and confident about who He was apart from titles. He was conscious of people, not positions. He was there to give, not gain.

- Security is the prerequisite to great undertakings. Only the secure will **STRETCH.**

- Security is the prerequisite to small undertakings. Only the secure will **STOOP.**

Servanthood begins with *security!*

Question: Are you secure enough to serve people without regard to your position?

3. INITIATE servant ministry to others. (John 13:4–5 MSG)

So he got up from the supper table, set aside his robe, and put on an apron. Then he poured water into a basin and began to wash the feet of the disciples, drying them with his apron.

Someone forgot to schedule the servant that night, and no one but Jesus volunteered for the job! Jesus initiated servant-leadership because no one else would. The following day, Pontius Pilate would pick up a basin of water and avoid responsibility. On this night, Jesus picked up a basin of water and assumed responsibility. He didn't wait for a "foot washing" rally to begin.

Question: Do you initiate acts of service to those under you?

Note Jesus' Attitude:

KEY POINTS

- He had nothing to **PROVE.** (Jesus didn't have to play games, project His self worth, or prove Himself to anyone.)

• He had nothing to **LOSE.** (Jesus didn't have to guard His reputation or fear He'd lose popularity. He took risks.)

• He had nothing to **HIDE.** (Jesus didn't keep up a facade or image for anyone. He was vulnerable, transparent.)

4. RECEIVE servant ministry from others. (John 13:6–8a MSG)

When he got to Simon Peter, Peter said, "Master, you wash my feet?" Jesus answered, "You don't understand now what I'm doing, but it will be clear enough to you later." Peter persisted, "You're not going to wash my feet—ever!"

Peter was still position-conscious at this point. This is why he couldn't receive from Jesus. True servants can receive ministry as well as give it, because they understand God's grace is what improves all service. They never want to stand in the way of grace-giving.

Question: Do you have too much pride to receive servant ministry from others?

5. Want nothing to interfere with their RELATIONSHIP with Jesus. (John 13:8b–9 MSG)

Jesus said, "If I don't wash you, you can't be part of what I'm doing." "Master," said Peter. "Not only my feet, then. Wash my hands! Wash my head!"

Peter moves from one extreme to the other. Why? He hungered to connect with Jesus. Once he realized it was OK for Jesus to wash him, he wanted an entire bath! He did everything with reckless abandon. It is love for God and for people that is behind a servant-leader's behavior. They respond quickly to God's connection in their lives.

Question: Do you hunger for intimacy with God so much that you'll do anything to get it?

6. Teach servanthood by their EXAMPLE. (John 13:12–15 MSG)

After he had finished washing their feet, he took his robe, put it back on, and went back to his place at the table. You address me as 'Teacher' and 'Master,' and rightly so. That is what I am. So if I, the Master and Teacher, washed your feet, you must now wash each other's feet. I've laid down a pattern for you."

#1 MOTIVATIONAL PRINCIPLE: PEOPLE DO WHAT PEOPLE SEE.

TRUTH IN A PICTURE

The Leadership Pyramid

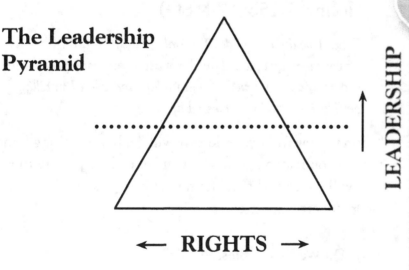

LEADERSHIP

← RIGHTS →

Observations

- Servant leaders don't gain rights as they reach the top—they surrender them.

- Everyone wants to be thought of as a servant, but no one wants to be treated like one.

- We would all love to wash Jesus' feet, but we are commanded to wash each other's feet.

- As Christians we are free in Christ; as leaders we must surrender freedoms for the sake of others (1 Cor. 9:19–22).

Question: Are you modeling what it means to surrender your rights as a leader?

7. Live a BLESSED life. (John 13:15b–17 MSG)

What I've done, you do. I'm only pointing out the obvious. A servant is not ranked above his master; an employee doesn't give orders to the employer. If you understand what I'm telling you, act like it—and live a blessed life.

"I don't know what your destiny will be, but one thing I know: the only ones among you who will be really happy are those who will have sought and found out how to serve."
—Dr. Albert Schweitzer

How Do We Live a Blessed Life?

When Jesus saw His ministry drawing huge crowds, He climbed a hillside. Those who were apprenticed to Him, the committed, climbed with Him. Arriving at a quiet place, He sat down and taught His climbing companions. This is what He said:

"You're blessed when you're at the end of your rope. With less of you there is more of God and his rule.

You're blessed when you feel you've lost what is most dear to you. Only then can you be embraced by the One most dear to you.

You're blessed when you're content with just who you are—no more, no less. That's the moment you find yourself proud owners of everything that can't be bought.

You're blessed when you've worked up a good appetite for God. He's food and drink in the best meal you'll ever eat.

You're blessed when you care. At the moment of being "carefull," you find yourselves cared for.

You're blessed when you get your inside world—your mind and heart—put right. Then you can see God in the outside world.

You're blessed when you can show people how to cooperate instead of compete or fight. That's when you discover who you really are, and your place in God's family.

You're blessed when your commitment to God provokes persecution. The persecution drives you even deeper into God's kingdom." (Matt. 5:3–10 MSG)

The Beatitudes in the Form of Personal Disciplines:

- Intentionally admit your need for God (Matt. 5:3).

- Be a person of brokenness before the Lord (Matt. 5:4).

- Give up your quest for personal rights (Matt. 5:5).

- Maintain a hunger and thirst for God (Matt. 5:6).

- Practice an identity with people in need (Matt. 5:7).

- Maintain a pure heart (Matt. 5:8).

- Cultivate peace in all relationships (Matt. 5:9).

- Take a positive view of criticism (Matt. 5:10).

Question: What blessings do you enjoy because of your decision to be a servant leader?

8. Live their lives OPPOSITE the philosophy of the world. (John 13:18 MSG)

I'm not including all of you in this. I know precisely whom I've selected, so as not to interfere with the fulfillment of this Scripture: The one who ate bread at my table turned his heel against me.

Don't push your way to the front; don't sweet-talk your way to the top. Put yourself aside, and help others get ahead. Don't be obsessed with getting your own advantage. Forget yourselves long enough to lend a helping hand. (Phil. 2:3–4 MSG)

CHECK YOUR HEART

Biblical Paradoxes

If I Want to . . .	I Must . . .	
save my life	lose my life	Luke 9:24–25
be lifted up	humble myself	James 4:10
be the greatest	be a servant.	Matthew 20:26–28
be first	be last.	Matthew 19:30
rule	serve	Luke 22:26–27
live	put to death the flesh.	Romans 8:13
be strong	be weak.	2 Corinthians 11:30
inherit the Kingdom	be poor in spirit	Matthew 5:3
reproduce	die	John 12:24

There are Seven Paths to Power:

1. Force (People have no choice.)

2. Intimidation (People are pushed.)

3. Manipulation (People are coerced.)

4. Exchange (People trade for something.)

5. Persuasion (People are convinced.)

6. Motivation (People act willingly.)

7. Honor (People are honored by their leader and they respond accordingly.)

Question: How is Jesus' leadership style different from Christian leaders' styles today?

_____

_____

_____

_____

ASSESSMENT: *On a scale of one to ten, how would you rate yourself as a leader who serves others?*

1   2   3   4   5   6   7   8   9   10

How do you believe others would rate you as a servant-leader?

1   2   3   4   5   6   7   8   9   10

ACTION PLAN

Courageous Leadership Workbook

APPLICATION: *Who is someone you find difficult to serve? List two ways you can serve them this week.*

_____

_____

_____

_____

_____

_____

The Life You Were Meant to Live

Lesson 7

Discovering Your God-given Mission in Life

Brethren, I do not regard myself as having laid hold of [the prize] yet; but one thing I do: forgetting what lies behind and reaching forward to what lies ahead, I press on toward the goal for the prize of the upward call of God in Christ Jesus. (Phil. 3:13–14 NASB)

Is it really possible for leaders to live their life on purpose? Is ministry merely about reacting to needs around us, or is it about something more? Can we play offense and not just defense with our lives? Does God have a specific mission for each of us to fulfill? The answer to each of these questions is yes, and in this exercise, you will receive the tools to live the life you were meant to live.

Five Biblical Foundations

1. We all have been given a PURPOSE for our lives.

2. We are most FULFILLED when we are fulfilling our purpose.

3. Not everyone UNCOVERS their God-given purpose.

4. Our purpose is BUILT from our personal inward design.

5. We will be JUDGED on our obedience to our God-given calling in life.

For the gifts and the calling of God are irrevocable. (Rom. 11:29 NASB)

Walk in a manner worthy of the calling with which you have been called. (Eph. 4:1 NASB)

How God Called Leaders in Scripture

In the Bible, we see at least four ways that God revealed someone's purpose in life. A calling unfolded just like it does for ordinary people like us today:

1. **THUNDERBOLT:** (Example: the Apostle Paul) God reveals your purpose in a moment or an event, and it becomes instantly clear.

2. **WALKING THROUGH OPEN DOORS:** (Example: Esther) God reveals your purpose over many years, step by step, as you capitalize on opportunities.

3. **THE CALL FROM BIRTH:** (Example: Jeremiah) God reveals your purpose early in life; you always remember being called.

4. **GROWING AWARENESS:** (Example: Joseph) God reveals your purpose in a general sense. As you move toward it, He provides the details.

Following in Jesus' Footsteps

Our Lord was very aware of His calling in life. Christ was given a purpose. We too, have been given a purpose. At the end of His life, Jesus prayed these words:

I glorified You on the earth, having accomplished the work which You have given Me to do. (John 17:4 NASB)

As the Father has sent Me, I also send you. (John 20:21b NASB)

CHECK YOUR HEART

Understanding Your Purpose

Earlier, we said our purposes are built from our personal inward designs. To understand your life's purpose, you should look inside your heart:

- **NATURAL TALENTS:** What abilities do you naturally possess?

- **SPIRITUAL GIFTS:** What are your primary motivational gifts?

- **INWARD DESIRES:** What do you really want to do?

- **RESULTS** and **FRUIT:** What produces the most when you do it?

- **AFFIRMATION** and **RECOGNITION:** What do friends affirm about you?

- **PASSION** and **CONVICTIONS:** What are you compelled to pursue?

- **FULFILLMENT** and **SATISFACTION:** What do you enjoy doing?

• **CIRCUMSTANCES** and **OPPORTUNITY:** What's in front of you now, as an opportunity?

Uncovering Your Life's Purpose

A second step toward understanding your life's purpose is to align yourself with God's purposes. Your purpose in life is not something you create but rather uncover. It is God-given and resides within every believer. The following are boundaries to make sure your purpose is God's idea, not merely your own.

Your Purpose Ought To . . .

1. **Begin with God's priorities.**

   It begins with His agenda, not yours: the Great Commandment and the Great Commission. Ask: "God, what are You doing in the world, and how can I join You?"

2. **Revolve around your identity.**

   Next, your purpose should reflect your answers to the list above, "Understanding Your Purpose." It will be unique to your gifts, passions, and desires.

3. **Include others.**

   God's purpose will not be fulfilled in isolation. It will always include people, and it will involve serving others. You cannot do it alone.

4. **Be bigger than yourself.**

   Your purpose will usually take a lifetime to fulfill. It will be God-sized. Richard Bach was asked how to know if our purpose is fulfilled. He stated, "If you're alive, it isn't."

5. Contain life-changing convictions.

Only if you have something worth living for do you really have something worth dying for. Your purpose should be about an activity for which you would give your life.

6. Have eternal value.

Eternity should be affected in some way by the fulfilling of your purpose. Don't limit it to simply moving things around here on earth. Make it count for eternity.

An Exercise for Writing Your Purpose Statement

The following is a list for life-planning. We suggest you take a day alone with God and respond to the ten items below. Use a separate sheet of paper, and take your time. From this list, begin to write a statement of purpose for your life.

CHECK YOUR HEART

• BURDENS

What needs tug most at your heart? What are the things that make you cry or make you angry or cause you to become passionate?

• HALLMARKS

What are the major hallmarks that have made up your life? List significant books, people, events, mentors, and accomplishments that have shaped your life so far.

• THEMES

What recurring themes or issues keep coming up in your conversations, sermons, or Bible studies you deliver? Are there subjects you return to regularly?

- ## TOOLS and RESOURCES

  What specific resources do you have at your side that you could employ as you fulfill your mission? These could be possessions, skills, or people to help you.

- ## STYLE

  What is your style of leadership, your personality, and your spiritual gifts? What unique means of influence do you use when you try to accomplish a task?

- ## DREAMS

  What are some of your aspirations or ideas that could be a God-given, clarified vision for the future? What are the things you'd love to do before you die?

- ## MISSION

  This is it. Begin to write out your purpose statement that answers the questions Why do I exist? and, Why did God give me to the world? Write out the central mission for your life in one to three sentences.

- ## VISION

  Based on your mission statement, describe in detail what you see as the ultimate results of your life, as if you could see your contribution from the other end of it. Start each vision statement with the words: "I see . . ."

- ## CORE VALUES

  Now list words that describe your deepest values. They should be principles that drive you. These values guide the decisions of your life and keep you on course. These should be simple, descriptive words. You should list no more than six.

• GOALS and OBJECTIVES

Finally, list the areas of your life (spiritual, family, professional, social) that are important to your purpose. List specific goals that will enable you to turn a lofty purpose statement into a practical "to do" list that you can begin to implement:

- Lifetime Goals: What do you want to do over your lifetime?

- Five-Year Goals: What do you want to see happen in three to five years?

- One-Year Goals: What do you want to do in the next year?

- 90-Day Goals: What will you do in the next three months?

- Next Steps: What steps will you take now in order to get started?

ACTION PLAN

APPLICATION: *Write out a statement of purpose based on the truths of this lesson.*

_____

_____

_____

_____

ASSESSMENT: *Find a Christian leader you believe is living his or her life on purpose. Locate someone you believe has a mature statement of purpose for his or her life. Ask, "How did you arrive at your purpose?"*

_____

_____

_____

_____

How Leaders Pray

Lesson 8
Praying Effectively in Pivotal Moments

*Now He was telling them a parable to show that at all
times they ought to pray and not to lose heart.*
(Luke 18:1 NASB)

Pivotal prayers come at pivotal moments. They produce
pivotal decisions and result in pivotal consequences.

Most people around the world pray. They do so because they
want God's help in tough times. Sadly, most never consider
how to pray about what is on God's heart, especially in
moments of trouble. Leaders understand the pivotal role of
prayer and pray strategically during key times. They don't panic
or simply react in fear. They seek and find God in moments
of stress and settle issues in prayer that lead to significant
breakthroughs in their lives and leadership.

It is easy to miss opportunities to pray a pivotal prayer.

How Do Leaders Seize Pivotal Moments in Prayer?

The Scripture tells us to "pray without ceasing" (1 Thess. 5:17
NASB). However, there are times when *what* we pray and
how we pray are more critical because of *when* we pray. The
moment introduces an opportunity for significant change.
Leaders recognize and seize such moments.

BIBLICAL
BASIS

Observations on How Leaders Pray

- **Effective leaders learn to THINK like God thinks and pray those thoughts.**

  Jesus demonstrated this in a pivotal moment. John 12 describes how Jesus faced the final hours of His earthly life. The reality of a painful, brutal cross loomed before Him. He was in anguish. Scripture tells us His emotions were so intense that He sweat "great drops of blood."

  So how did Jesus pray? Recognizing the pivotal moment, He prayed,

  > *Now My soul has become troubled; and what shall I say, "Father, save Me from this hour"? But for this purpose I came to this hour. Father, glorify Your name.* (John 12:27–28a NASB)

  Did you notice Jesus contemplated what kind of prayer to pray? He could have prayed a survival prayer: "Father, get Me out of this mess!" That would have been natural. It might have been what we would have prayed. Instead, Jesus aligned His prayer with His Father's ultimate purposes. The result: the redemption of the world. Key moment. Key prayer. Key decision. Key results.

- **Effective leaders pray from RELATIONSHIP, not just routine.**

  Pivotal prayers move past clichés and unthinking phrases to meaningful exchanges with God. It means we pray from our hearts, not just our heads. We aren't concerned with image but substance. It's the kind of prayer experience we say we want but seldom practice.

How often are our prayer lives reduced to meaningless, routine monologues? Or to time constraints or image-seeking when we pray publicly? If many of us were to get honest, we'd admit our prayer life borders on superstition. We go through the motions, speaking a few worn-out phrases to make sure God is on our side before we head into our day.

- **Effective leaders learn pivotal prayer as they MATURE spiritually.**

We learn to pray this way over time. Pivotal praying increases as we mature spiritually. Leaders often become caught up in fulfilling their agenda. Mature leaders trade their agenda for God's. They move from simply praying what *they* want, to praying with God's larger vision in mind.

This was vividly illustrated in the story of three missionaries. In 1993, three New Tribes Mission missionaries were kidnapped in Colombia by terrorists. For eight long years their families and friends wondered and prayed and worried. Eventually they were informed that the men were dead. Dan Germann, who was the NTM director in Colombia at that time, said in an interview that their prayers changed through those long years of uncertainty. They started out praying that God would bring the men home safely. They ended up praying, "God, even if we never know what has become of them, You will still be God." Dan said, "There is a very special sense of awe at who God is and how sufficient He is when the miracle doesn't happen, but the wonder of His sufficiency is still present. This too is the triumph of grace. We come to realize that God is *God* . . . His cause is the one cause on the face of the earth that will finally succeed."

101

Learning to pray this way isn't a cop-out. It doesn't mean we stop trusting God to do miracles and leave it to fate. It means we trust Him and His purposes regardless of our understanding.

- **Effective leaders recognize CRITICAL moments and pray strategically.**

Leaders perceive key junctions in their lives and pray wisely in those times. They see beyond their own personal interests. There is nothing wrong with praying for personal needs or for current circumstances. However, when we forget the ultimate, we become a slave to the immediate.

CHECK YOUR HEART

Three Levels of Prayer

During times of war, we hear the military terms "logistical," "tactical," and "strategic" initiatives. While these terms describe three levels of military operations, they also describe three levels of prayer.

1. **LOGISTICAL PRAYER**

   The focus is on our own personal needs. It is prayed from a temporal perspective. If we were to pray before we lead the Sunday morning worship service, and we prayed a logistical prayer, we might say, "Lord, help us to do well this morning. Help us to finish our service on time, help the microphones to work, and help us to be calm. Amen."

2. **TACTICAL PRAYER**

   The focus is on helping others, but is still prayed from a temporal perspective. If we were to pray this kind of prayer before our Sunday morning worship service, we might say: "Lord, please bless all who participate in the service today, and bless the people who attend. May it be inspiring to everyone. Amen." This prayer is better than the first one but it still doesn't fully capture God's heart and purposes for the world.

3. STRATEGIC PRAYER

The focus is on God's ultimate objectives for the world. It is prayed from an eternal perspective. It captures His heart and purpose rather than mere human purposes. If we pray strategically before our worship service, we might say: "Lord, raise up disciples from this service today. Regardless of what happens to the microphones, the musicians, or anyone else on the platform, use this service to glorify Yourself and bring Your Kingdom more fully to this earth. Amen."

An Example from the Bible . . .

EXAMINE THE WORD

Second Kings 3:5–18 tells the story of the army of Israel just before they faced the Moabites in battle. It was one more illustration of God's people missing a pivotal moment because they were caught up in themselves. Ancient Israel and two allies took their armies through the wilderness to face the Moabite army. After a week, however, they faced a crisis: they ran out of water.

They decided to go to the prophet Elisha to seek God's help. They begged for water. As the prophet sought the Lord, He responded through Elisha and said in essence, "I will give you water, but this is a small thing for Me. I will also give the Moabites into your hands!"

Sound familiar? In this pivotal moment Israel asked for the wrong thing. They saw only the small picture. They only sought the solution to their immediate needs. They prayed

Courageous Leadership Workbook

a logistical prayer. They prayed for the water, not the war! Pivotal praying means we perceive crucial moments and how the future hinges on them.

- ## Effective leaders learn to pray UNSELFISHLY.

  The fact is most people pray, but most of us pray selfishly. In 1993 a survey was conducted among two thousand church attendees asking questions about their prayer habits. If their answers are any reflection of the general population, we have a lot of room to grow. The top three prayer subjects of those surveyed were meals, personal and family safety, and personal blessings. The average person spent less than seven minutes a day in prayer.

  I am not saying this is evil, only that it is limited in potential. God yearns to accomplish so much more through our prayers, if we can only get on the same page He's on! Based upon your prayer life today, how would you do if you faced a pivotal moment?

- ## Effective leaders don't pursue eloquence, but simply CONNECT with God's heart.

  Pivotal prayer has more to do with the posture of your heart when you pray than the words you choose. It is the expression of your heart aligned with God's heart to fulfill His purposes in your circumstance. It may also be the difference between connecting and not connecting with God. Not all prayers connect with Him. Do you remember the publican and the Pharisee in Luke 18:10–14? One connected with God; the other didn't, even though his words were beautiful.

CHECK YOUR HEART

- **Effective leaders learn to pray from MISSION, not maintenance.**

Perhaps this is the top reason why leaders need to understand pivotal praying. It means staying focused on the mission, even in crisis; staying in relationship with God when it is easier to pray out of familiar routines; playing offense, not merely defense in our prayer time.

Think with me for a moment about Jesus in Gethsemane. If there was ever a moment He was tempted to shift into idle and pray a logistical prayer, it was in the Garden of Gethsemane. Hours away from torture and death, Jesus considers the temptation: "My Father, if it is possible, may this cup pass from Me." This is a normal reaction to His situation. However, He then added a strategic phrase: "yet not as I will, but as You will" (Matt. 26:39 NASB). It was a pivotal moment. Jesus stayed on mission in His prayer.

Courageous Leadership Workbook

ACTION PLAN

ASSESSMENT: *Think of a recent crisis you've experienced. What was the first request you prayed? How did your prayer reflect the heart of God and the importance of the moment?*

_____

_____

_____

_____

APPLICATION: *Consider that same crisis, and take a moment now to pray a pivotal prayer.*

_____

_____

_____

_____

Discovering Your Spiritual Gifts

Lesson 9

Identifying Your Primary Gift and Role in the Body of Christ

As each one has received a special gift, employ it in serving one another as good stewards of the manifold grace of God. (1 Pet. 4:10 NASB)

BIBLICAL BASIS

One of the most important discoveries you will make as a Christian leader is the discovery of the gifts that God has placed inside you as a believer. These gifts, or spiritual abilities, are given to every believer. They are to be discovered, developed, and distributed for the purpose of serving others. May this lesson be an encouragement to you as you discover your most fruitful role in the body of Christ. Our focus will be the primary (or motivational) gifts listed in Romans 12.

A Foundation for Spiritual Gifts (Rom. 12:3–8)

The foundational truth of this passage is that God has placed a primary gift inside every believer. This gift will play an important role in how you approach your leadership position. Before we examine the details of the passage, let's establish a foundation for spiritual gifts:

- The New Testament lists a wide **VARIETY** of spiritual gifts (1 Cor. 12:4–11, Eph. 4:11–16, 1 Pet. 4:10–11, Rom. 12:3–8).

- Each Christian has a **PRIMARY GIFT** on which they should focus their time (Rom. 12:6–8).

- The Holy Spirit wants to supernaturally reveal **JESUS** through these gifts (John 16:13–15).

- Like muscles in our body, gifts can be present but **UNDEVELOPED** (1 Cor. 12:12–16).

- Every one of these gifts is important and has a **FUNCTION.** Each works like a position on a team or a muscle in the body (1 Cor. 12:18–25).

- God's primary **PURPOSE** for them is to advance His Kingdom (Eph. 4:11–13).

Motivational Gifts

In Romans 12:3–8, we read about these primary gifts:

- **The Gift of Prophecy:** declaring God's truth concerning present and future direction

- **The Gift of Service:** ministering to others by meeting whatever needs they have

- **The Gift of Teaching:** equipping the body of Christ to know and obey God

- **The Gift of Exhortation:** sharing words of encouragement; challenging others to act

- **The Gift of Giving:** generously sharing resources so that God's work can advance

- **The Gift of Leadership:** providing vision, direction, and empowerment to others

- **The Gift of Mercy:** demonstrating God's grace to those who struggle or suffer

While most leaders have a cluster of spiritual gifts, we believe each leader has one primary gift that brings the most value to the body of Christ. The cluster of gifts could be called a gift-set. The primary gift becomes the center of the wheel around which the other gifts revolve.

For instance, one leader might have the gift of teaching. In addition, he might also possess the gift of administration and the gift of helps (1 Cor. 12:28). Those gifts may serve to influence the way this leader does his teaching, but the teaching will likely be the primary gift in his life. This means, regardless of the ministry position he may possess in the future, somewhere in his work will be the act of teaching. The key is to find your primary gift.

Don't Be Confused

It is easy to become confused about spiritual gifts. There are counterfeits that appear to be gifts, but they are not. Don't confuse spiritual gifts with . . .

KEY POINTS

- ## NATURAL TALENTS.

    Most of us possess natural talents as well as spiritual gifts. We receive natural talents at our first birth, our natural birth. We receive spiritual gifts at our second birth, our spiritual birth. Atheists have natural talents, but they do not possess spiritual gifts. Both are abilities that are God-given, but the sole purpose for spiritual gifts is not to make money or entertain people but to advance God's rule and reign on earth.

111

- ## FRUIT OF THE SPIRIT.

  There is a difference between the fruit of the Spirit and the gifts of the Spirit. God determines what gifts we possess. We determine what fruit we will bear, based on our obedience and faithfulness. We will be judged by the fruit we bore, not the volume of our gifts. Gifts are temporal, but fruit is forever. Don't compare or judge others' gifts; that is up to God. We should be focusing on bearing fruit and glorifying our Father in heaven.

- ## CHRISTIAN ROLES.

  Although every believer has a primary gift, we are all called to fulfill the roles of evangelism, prayer, and giving. Some Christians may do more evangelism than others because they are gifted in that area, but all of us are called to be witnesses. We cannot say: "I cannot do that, it is not my gift." We all must give of our money and pray for others, even if we don't have the gifts of giving or intercession.

- ## COUNTERFEIT GIFTS.

  Be careful. The enemy is at work, and he will counterfeit these gifts. That's how we know they are important. A criminal only counterfeits money because he knows it is valuable! Beware of what Jesus spoke of in Matthew 7:22–23. He said that many will come to Him on the judgment day boasting about the ministry they did, but they are counterfeits. He will say: "I never knew you." All of our gifts should operate out of a loving relationship with Jesus Christ.

Have You Discovered Your Gift?

You will not discover or develop your gift if . . .

. . . there remains an unresolved difference between you and God.

. . . you never step out and do something in obedience to God.

. . . you are attempting to imitate someone else's gift.

. . . you are constantly living in the flesh.

Are You a Thief? (1 Pet. 4:7–11)

We must take the risk of using our gifts in ministry. If we don't, we fail to obey God. In this passage we are commanded to employ our gifts to serve people. If we fail to step out and do so, there are three results:

• You rob **YOURSELF** of being in God's will (v. 10).

• You rob the **BODY OF CHRIST** of the benefit of that gift (v. 10).

• You rob **GOD** of the glory He deserves (v. 11).

Steps to Discover and Develop Your Gifts

1. EXPLORE the possibilities.

CHECK YOUR HEART

Get familiar with what Scripture teaches on spiritual gifts, and recognize that your gift may be the way God will allow you to impact your world in the most profound way.

Ask yourself, "Do I understand the New Testament gifts and opportunities available?"

2. EXPERIMENT as much as possible.

Allow the church to be a laboratory where you and others can experiment with your gifts as you serve others. Make it a safe place for people to try out ministry opportunities.

Ask yourself, "Am I doing something to discover my calling and gifts?"

3. EXAMINE how you feel.

When you try some new ministry, are you fulfilled doing it? Do you sense that it fits your abilities and skills? Does it satisfy you down in your soul?

Ask yourself, "Am I fulfilled in what I am doing?"

4. EVALUATE your effectiveness.

As you reflect on what you did, using your gifts, how did you do? Were you good at it? Did you see any fruit borne? Did you get results and see God's Kingdom move forward?

Ask yourself, "Am I good at the ministry I am doing? Are there results?"

5. EXPECT confirmation from the body of Christ.

As you serve, do other Christians confirm that you are gifted in that area? What do the mature members of the body of Christ say as they watch you serve? Listen for the response of others.

Ask yourself, "Do the Christians around me recognize this strength in me?"

Conclusion . . .

Remember—God would never place a gift inside you and then tell you to let it sit dormant. If He gives you any resources (time, talents, money), He expects you to use them (Matt. 25:14–30). If you are serving now in some ministry but do not sense fulfillment or do not see fruit or don't hear any confirmation from others that your ministry fits you well—stay alert. You may have yet to find the place where your gifts lie. When you find your gifts, you will see fruit for God's Kingdom, and inside your heart you will sense, *this is what I was built to do!*

ACTION PLAN

ASSESSMENT: *Based on this lesson, what do you believe is your primary spiritual gift?*

_____

_____

_____

_____

How and where do you believe you can best use it?

_____

_____

_____

_____

APPLICATION: *Use the Spiritual Gifts Discovery Tool on the next few pages of this notebook. Which are your top three gifts? Next, follow the five steps above and experiment with those gifts. What do you discover when you follow the five steps?*

_____

_____

_____

_____

_____

Spiritual Gifts Discovery Tool

This is not a test, so enjoy the process! There are no right or wrong answers—only true facts about your experience and preference according to the following statements.

1. Read the seventy-two statements, rating each one from zero to four on the answer key.

   • Remember that 0 isn't "bad" and 4 isn't "good." It is simply a reflection of where your strengths are.

   • When you find a statement with two or more parts, and you rate any one as not true in your life, then mark the whole question with a low number. In other words, if you think one part is true, but another part is not, rate the whole question with a low number.

2. Add up the eighteen rows of four numbers and enter the totals in the "total" column.

3. Find your three to five highest scores and circle the appropriate letters (A to R) by the high scores.

4. Turn to the "Gifts Key" page and find the eighteen gifts listed from A to R.

   • On your answer sheet, write in the name of the gifts corresponding with your high scores.

   • There is not a specific number needed to "get the gift!" Your highest scores indicate which gifts are yours. For example, if you have two 7s, an 8, and two 9s as your highest scores, then those are your gifts. If you have four 16s, those are your gifts.

- You may wish to write in all eighteen gift names on your answer sheet to compare your strong gifts with those that are not your strongest.

5. Talk to your pastor or supervisor about which ministries match your gifts.

> We understand that some Christian movements recognize more spiritual gifts in the Bible and some recognize less. We recommend that you work within the boundaries of your denomination or movement and develop your spiritual gifts for the glory of God.

Spiritual Gifts Discovery

1. I enjoy working behind the scenes, taking care of little details.

2. I usually step forward and assume leadership in a group where none exists.

3. When in a group, I tend to notice those who are alone and help them feel part of the group.

4. I have the ability to recognize a need and to get the job done, no matter how small the task.

5. I have the ability to organize ideas, people, and projects to reach a specific goal.

6. People often say I have good spiritual judgment.

7. I am very confident of achieving great things for the glory of God.

8. I enjoy giving money to those in serious financial need.

9. I enjoy ministering to people in hospitals, prisons, or rest homes to comfort them.

10. I often have insights that offer practical solutions to difficult problems.

11. I enjoy encouraging and giving counsel to those who are discouraged.

12. I have an ability to thoroughly study a passage of Scripture and then share it with others.

13. I presently have the responsibility for the spiritual growth of one or more young Christians.

14. Other people respect me as an authority in spiritual matters.

15. I have an ability to learn foreign languages.

16. God often reveals to me the direction He desires the body of Christ to move.

17. I enjoy developing relationships with non-Christians with the hope of telling them about Jesus.

18. Whenever I hear about needy situations, I am burdened to pray.

19. I would like to assist pastors or other leaders so they can focus on their priority ministries.

20. When I ask people to help me with an important ministry for the church, they usually say yes.

21. I enjoy entertaining guests and making them feel "at home" when they visit.

22. I take initiative to serve and I enjoy serving others, no matter how small the task.

23. I am a very organized person who sets goals, makes plans, and achieves them both.

24. I am a good judge of character and can spot a spiritual phony.

25. I often step out and start projects that other people won't attempt, and I usually succeed.

26. I joyfully give money well above my tithe to the church.

27. I feel compassion for people who are hurting and lonely, and I like to spend considerable time with them to cheer them up.

28. God has enabled me to choose correctly between several complex options in an important decision, when no one else knew what to do.

29. I am very fulfilled when I encourage others, especially if it is about their spiritual growth.

30. I enjoy studying difficult questions about God's Word, and I usually find the answers quickly.

31. I enjoy being involved in people's lives and helping them grow spiritually.

32. I would be willing and excited to start a new church.

33. I can adapt easily to cultures, languages, and lifestyles other than my own, and I would like to use my adaptability to minister in foreign countries.

34. I will always speak up for Christian principles with conviction, even when it isn't popular.

35. I find it easy to invite a person to accept Jesus as their Savior.

36. I have a passion to pray for the significant issues of God's Kingdom and His will for Christians.

37. I enjoy relieving others of routine tasks so they can get important projects done.

38. I can guide and motivate a group of people toward achieving a specific goal.

39. I enjoy meeting new people and introducing them to others in the group.

40. I am very dependable for getting things done on time, and I don't need much praise or thanks.

41. I easily delegate significant responsibilities to other people.

42. I am able to distinguish between right and wrong in complex spiritual matters when other people can't seem to figure it out.

43. I trust in God's faithfulness for a bright future even when facing significant problems.

44. I wouldn't mind lowering my standard of living to give more to the church and others in need.

45. I want to do whatever I can for the needy people around me, even if I have to give up something.

46. People often seek my advice when they don't know what to do in a situation.

47. I feel a need to challenge others to better themselves, especially in their spiritual growth, in an uplifting rather than condemning way.

48. Others listen to and enjoy my teaching of Scriptures.

49. I care about the spiritual welfare of people and do my best to guide others toward a godly lifestyle.

50. I am accepted as a spiritual authority in other parts of the country or world.

51. I would like to present the gospel in a foreign language, in a country different than my own.

52. I feel a need to speak God's biblical messages so people will know what God expects of them.

53. I like to tell others how to become a Christian and invite them to receive Jesus into their life.

54. Many of my prayers for others have been answered by the Lord.

55. I enjoy helping others get their work done, and I don't need a lot of public recognition.

56. People respect my opinion and follow my direction.

57. I would like to use my home to get acquainted with newcomers and visitors to the church.

58. I enjoy helping people in any type of need and feel a sense of satisfaction in meeting that need.

59. I am comfortable making important decisions, even under pressure.

60. People come to me for help in distinguishing between spiritual truth and error.

61. I often exercise my faith through prayer, and God answers my prayers in powerful ways.

62. When I give money to someone, I don't expect anything in return, and I often give anonymously.

63. When I hear of people without jobs who can't pay their bills, I do what I can to help them.

64. God enables me to make appropriate application of biblical truth to practical situations.

65. People respond well to my encouragement to become all they can be for God.

66. I am systematic in my approach to presenting Bible lessons to a group of people.

67. I help Christians who have wandered away from the Lord find their way back to a growing relationship with Him and get involved in a local church.

68. I would be excited to share the gospel and form new groups of Christians in areas where there aren't many churches.

69. I have no racial prejudice and have a sincere appreciation for people very different from myself.

70. I find it relatively easy to apply biblical promises to present day situations, and I'm willing to confront in love, if necessary.

71. I have a strong desire to help non-Christians find salvation through Jesus Christ.

72. Prayer is my favorite ministry in the church, and I consistently spend a great deal of time at it.

NOTES

Answer Key

Select the value from 0–4 that indicates the statement's truth in your life.

   0 – Not at all

   1 – Little

   2 – Moderately

   3 – Considerably

   4 – Strongly

For best results, do not review the Gift Key until you have answered all the statements.

Answers				Total	Row	Gift
1. ___	19. ___	37. ___	55. ___	_____	A	_____
2. ___	20. ___	38. ___	56. ___	_____	B	_____
3. ___	21. ___	39. ___	57. ___	_____	C	_____
4. ___	22. ___	40. ___	58. ___	_____	D	_____
5. ___	23. ___	41. ___	59. ___	_____	E	_____
6. ___	24. ___	42. ___	60. ___	_____	F	_____
7. ___	25. ___	43. ___	61. ___	_____	G	_____
8. ___	26. ___	44. ___	62. ___	_____	H	_____
9. ___	27. ___	45. ___	63. ___	_____	I	_____
10. ___	28. ___	46. ___	64. ___	_____	J	_____
11. ___	29. ___	47. ___	65. ___	_____	K	_____
12. ___	30. ___	48. ___	66. ___	_____	L	_____
13. ___	31. ___	49. ___	67. ___	_____	M	_____
14. ___	32. ___	50. ___	68. ___	_____	N	_____
15. ___	33. ___	51. ___	69. ___	_____	O	_____
16. ___	34. ___	52. ___	70. ___	_____	P	_____
17. ___	35. ___	53. ___	71. ___	_____	Q	_____
18. ___	36. ___	54. ___	72. ___	_____	R	_____

GIFTS KEY: A–R Definitions and Scriptural References

While not meant to be dogmatic or final, these definitions and supporting Scriptures do correspond to characteristics of the gifts as expressed in the Spiritual Gifts Discovery Tool.

EXAMINE THE WORD

A. Helps: the ability to work with and support other Christians' ministry efforts
   - Mark 15:40–41
   - Romans 16:1–2
   - Acts 9:36
   - 1 Corinthians 12:28

B. Leadership: the ability to influence others according to a "big picture" purpose, mission, or plan
   - Romans 12:8
   - 1 Timothy 5:17
   - 1 Timothy 3:1–13
   - Hebrews 13:17

C. Hospitality: the ability to make people feel "at home," welcome, cared for, and part of the group
   - Acts 16:14–15
   - 1 Peter 4:9
   - Hebrews 13:1–2
   - Romans 12:13
   - Romans 16:23

D. Service: the ability to identify and meet the practical needs of others
   - Acts 6:1–7
   - Titus 3:14
   - 2 Timothy 1:16–18
   - Romans 12:7
   - Galatians 6:10

E. Administration: the ability to coordinate and organize people and projects
   - Luke 14:28–30
   - 1 Corinthians 12:28
   - Acts 6:1–7

F. Discernment: the ability to perceive whether a person's actions originate from godly, satanic, or merely human sources
   - Matthew 16:21–23
   - 1 John 4:1–6
   - 1 Corinthians 12:10
   - Acts 5:1–11
   - Acts 16:16–18

G. Faith: the ability to believe God with confidence for things unseen, for spiritual growth, and for the acceptance of the will of God
   - Acts 11:22–24
   - 1 Corinthians 12:9
   - Romans 4:18–21
   - Hebrews 11

H. Giving: the ability to cheerfully and generously contribute personal resources to God's work
   - Mark 12:41–44
   - 2 Corinthians 8:1–7
   - Romans 12:8
   - 2 Corinthians 9:2–7

I. Mercy: the ability to feel sincere empathy and compassion in a way that results in practical relief for people's hurts, pain, and suffering
   - Matthew 9:35–36
   - Romans 12:8
   - Mark 9:41
   - 1 Thessalonians 5:14

J. Wisdom: the ability to discern the mind of Christ and apply Scriptural truth to a specific situation in order to make the right choices and help others move in the right direction
   - Acts 6:3, 10
   - 1 Corinthians 12:8
   - 1 Corinthians 2:6–13

K. Exhortation: the ability to appropriately communicate words of encouragement, challenge, or rebuke in the body of Christ
   - Acts 14:22
   - 1 Timothy 4:13
   - Romans 12:8
   - Hebrews 10:24–25

L. Teaching: the ability to employ a logical, systematic approach to biblical study in preparation for clearly communicating practical truth to the body of Christ
- Acts 18:24–28
- Acts 20:20–21
- 1 Corinthians 12:28
- Ephesians 4:11–14

M. Pastoring/Shepherding: the ability to assume responsibility for the spiritual growth and Christian community of a group of believers
- John 10:1–18
- Ephesians 4:11–14
- 1 Timothy 3:1–7
- 1 Peter 5:1–3

N. Apostleship: the ability to pioneer ministries and to provide spiritual leadership over a number of churches that results in fruitful ministry
- Acts 15:22–35
- 1 Corinthians 12:28
- Ephesians 4:11–14
- 2 Corinthians 12:12
- Galatians 2:7–10

O. Missions: the ability to minister effectively in cultures beyond your own
- Acts 8:4
- Acts 13:2–3
- Acts 22:21
- Romans 10:15

P. Prophecy: the ability to boldly declare the truth of God, regardless of the consequences, calling people to righteous living
- Acts 2:37–40
- Acts 7:51–53
- 1 Thessalonians 1:5
- Acts 26:24–29
- 1 Corinthians 14:1–4

Q. Evangelism: the ability to share the good news of Jesus Christ with others in such a way that many non-Christians believe in Christ and are converted to Christianity
- Acts 8:5–6
- Acts 8:26–40
- Ephesians 4:11–14
- Acts 14:21
- Acts 21:8

R. Intercession: the ability to pray for significant lengths of time on a regular basis, often observing specific answers to those prayers
- Colossians 1:9–12
- Colossians 4:12–13
- James 5:14–16

Adapted from *Spiritual Gifts, A Tool to Discover Your Place in Ministry* by Dan Reiland, copyright INJOY, Inc., 1998, Atlanta, GA.

I Like Your Style!

Lesson 10

Choosing Your Leadership Style

Conduct yourselves with wisdom toward outsiders, making the most of the opportunity. Let your speech always be with grace, as though seasoned with salt, so that you will know how you should respond to each person. (Col. 4:5–6 NASB)

BIBLICAL BASIS

All leaders influence people, but they do it differently. As a leader, one of the most important discoveries you can make is how you influence others most effectively for the Kingdom of God. Every leader has been created uniquely by God. You must find your unique leadership style and employ it for God's glory.

Leaders Influence People in Different Ways Because of . . .

- PERSONALITY
- TIMING
- ORGANIZATION
- TRADITION
- CULTURE
- THE ISSUE

Leadership Style Statements:

- There is not just one right way to **LEAD.**

- Great leaders will change styles, but not **PRINCIPLES.**

- Lasting leaders determine their style by observing their **PEOPLE**.

Discussion: Which is correct? Effective leadership is taking people from where they are to where . . .

> . . . you want them to be.

> . . . they want to be.

> . . . they need to be.

"True leadership must be for the benefit of the followers, not the enrichment of the leaders." —Robert Townsend

"A leader takes people where they want to go. A great leader takes people where they don't necessarily want to go, but ought to be." —Rosalyn Carter

Five Different Styles of Leaders

1. DOMINATING STYLE

This style can be overpowering and must be combined with love. This style of leader gets others to do things simply because he or she wants it done. The leader is strong and sometimes forceful. He or she is often known as "the boss."

Characteristics of Dominators

- Intimidating
- Controlling of others
- One-way communication
- Strong will and personality
- Require blind obedience
- Negative

An On-going Dominating Style Will Cause:

- Resentment from followers

- High turnover, as people will leave the organization

- A fearful climate and average production

How to Work for a Dominator

- **FOLLOW** directions.

- Never let him or her **DEVALUE** you.

- Mind your **OWN** business.

- Find the **KEY** to his or her life.

- Don't take things **PERSONALLY.**

- Get another **MINISTRY** position.

2. NEGOTIATING STYLE

This style is easier to follow. This person discusses what needs to be done and gets others to join him or her because both the leader and the follower want it done. He or she works toward cooperation without diminishing his or her goals.

"The Law of Connection:
Leaders touch a heart
before they ask for a hand."
—Dr. John C. Maxwell

Courageous Leadership Workbook

Ten Negotiating Principles

1. The ideal result of negotiating is win-win-win (leader, follower, team).

2. Start negotiations with high expectations.

3. Know what you want to achieve before negotiating.

4. Know what you won't stand for before negotiating (for example: bad attitudes, distrust, threats, secrets, closed minds).

5. Separate the person from the issue.

6. Discover beforehand what the other person really wants.

7. Generate a variety of possibilities before deciding what to do.

8. Don't match concessions one for one.

9. Weigh carefully offers you've never considered before.

10. Have a time limit and tangible way to evaluate the decision.

3. PERSUADING STYLE

This style is smooth and often full of charisma. This leader is personable and considers what the follower wants. In fact, this style gets others to do things because the follower wants it. He or she is convincing to followers. The word "persuasion" comes from two root words meaning "through sweetness."

Principles of Persuasion

- **PASSION** is foundational.
- **INTEGRITY** is fundamental.
- **CONFIDENCE** is essential.
- **PERSPECTIVE** is beneficial.
- **DISCERNMENT** is critical.
- **LOVE** is motivational.

People don't care how much you know until they know how much you care. Aristotle spoke of three ingredients of persuasion:

- Logos = Reason
- Pathos = Emotion
- Ethos = Credibility

4. MODELING STYLE

This is a convincing style because the leader never asks the followers to do something that he has not done himself. He gets others to do things because the follower sees it. He leads by example. This leader knows that you cannot lead others farther than where you have gone yourself.

The Equipping Process

1. **MODELING:** The leader does it.

2. **MENTORING:** The leader does it and the follower watches.

3. **MONITORING:** The follower does it and the leader watches.

4. **MOTIVATING:** The follower does it.

5. MULTIPLYING: The follower does it and someone else watches.

5. EMPOWERING STYLE

This is the most effective way of leading long term. This is where the leader gets others to do things because he or she feels they are capable. The leader gives his power away and, therefore, multiplies his leadership. Pittacus said, "The measure of a man is what he does with power."

Characteristics of Leaders Who Empower:

a.	Their vision is bigger than they are.	e.	They have servants' hearts.
b.	They believe in people.	f.	They are transparent.
c.	They have an excellent self-image.	g.	They are highly successful.
d.	They are people-developers.	h.	They have God's anointing.

The danger of power lies in the fact that those who have it tend to make its preservation their first concern. Such people are reluctant to relinquish the privileges that power brings to them. It is impossible to hold on to power and at the same time give it to others. Those who draw lines, declare authority, and fight for their own rights soon see their power diminish. Only those who pass it on to others find their power increases. To empower others is to empower yourself.

Five Leadership Styles: What to Expect from Them

STYLE	REQUIRES	POSITIVE	NEGATIVE
Dominating	Blind obedience	Immediate action	Negative reaction
Negotiating	Mutual victory	Entrepreneurship	Unequal effort
Persuading	Motivational skills	Winning attitude	Leader dependence
Modeling	Time together	Loyalty	When leader falls
Empowering	Anointing	Extraordinary living	Too much reliance on leader's blessing

ASSESSMENT: *Which leadership style do you employ?*

ACTION PLAN

_____

_____

_____

_____

_____

APPLICATION: *Identify a situation this week and choose the best style to lead in that situation. Discuss this with a colleague.*

_____

_____

_____

_____

_____

How to Grow a Leader

Lesson 11

What It Takes to Develop Other Leaders in Your Organization

BIBLICAL BASIS

Shepherd the flock of God among you, exercising oversight not under compulsion, but voluntarily, according to the will of God; and not for sordid gain, but with eagerness; nor yet as lording it over those allotted to your charge, but proving to be examples to the flock. (1 Pet. 5:2–3 NASB)

A leader who develops followers ADDS.

A leader who develops leaders MULTIPLIES.

How to Grow a Leader

1. **DISCERN:** It takes one to know one. True leaders can identify other leaders.
2. **DEMONSTRATE:** It takes one to show one. True leaders are models.
3. **DEVELOP:** It takes one to grow one. True leaders equip other leaders.

"The Law of Reproduction:
It takes a leader to develop a leader."
—Dr. John C. Maxwell

2 Timothy 2:1–26

So why don't we do it? Why do leaders not develop more leaders? Because it is hard work! Note the pictures the Apostle Paul gives us for the task of leadership:

EXAMINE
THE
WORD

- **TRAINER**

  We are to train and equip faithful men to do what we have done (vv. 1–2).

- **SOLDIER**

  We are to endure hardship and stay focused on our mission (vv. 3–4).

- **ATHLETE**

  We are to be disciplined and lead others with integrity (v. 5).

- **FARMER**

  We are to work hard like farmers, growing the people in our care (vv. 6–7).

- **WORKER**

  We are to study and labor to handle God's Word accurately (v. 15).

- **VESSEL**

  We are to stay pure so God can use us for His highest purposes (vv. 20–21).

- **BONDSERVANT**

  We are to submit and stay humble, being kind to all people (vv. 24–26).

Effective leadership is not an easy task, and the most challenging task of all the leadership tasks is to grow more leaders. Potential leaders are challenging to find; they are challenging to guide; they are challenging to train—but we must do it. The future of the church will be impacted by our ability to grow more and better leaders! So, the issue is not *addition* to the church, but *multiplication*.

Leaders Who Develop Followers	Leaders Who Develop Leaders
• Insecure	• Secure
• Vision no bigger than self	• Vision bigger than self
• Selfish	• Unselfish
• Natural leader	• Learned leadership
• Chief enjoyment: praise of others	• Chief enjoyment: growth of others

How to Identify a Leader

Potential leaders will . . .

- **INFLUENCE OTHERS.**

  This is the most consistent fact about leaders. Note who they influence, how many they influence, and when they influence others.

- **CHALLENGE THE PROCESS.**

  They are hungry to make things better and are willing to change. They enjoy making progress and become restless when things remain static.

- **BE DRIVEN BY A VISION.**

  They can get others excited about their dreams. The person with a vision talks little but does a lot. They have a fire inside of them to fulfill a dream.

- **RELATE WELL WITH PEOPLE.**

  Leaders will not experience long-term success unless a lot of people support them. Potential leaders have learned the value of people and can connect with them.

- **WORK WELL UNDER PRESSURE.**

  Their value lies in what they can do and what they can endure. You will notice potential leaders have the ability to thrive under pressure.

- **SOLVE PROBLEMS WELL.**

  You can judge a leader by the size of the problems he handles. People almost always pick a problem their own size.

- **COMMUNICATE EFFECTIVELY.**

  When they communicate, they get people to think, feel, and act differently.

- **BE CONFIDENT.**

  Potential leaders believe they can make a difference and want to prove it.

- **POSSESS A POSITIVE ATTITUDE.**

  Leadership has more to do with attitude than position. Potential leaders have a positive attitude, a servant's attitude, and a persistent attitude.

- **WANT TO BE EVALUATED BY RESULTS.**

  Leaders want to be respected for their production, not their position.

Questions to Ask Yourself Before You Grow a Leader

- Is my life an example for others to follow?

- Am I willing to pour my life into another?

- How will I pass on my strengths to another?

- What is the potential of the one I choose?

- Are we compatible in personality and mission?

- What type of person does this potential leader influence now?

CHECK
YOUR
HEART

Seven Steps to Developing Leaders

1. CHOOSE THEM WISELY.

When selecting potential leaders to develop, choose people with great:

- Desire to make a difference. (They must be hungry to grow.)

- Potential to make a difference. (A "5" will not lead a "10.")

Who are some potential leaders you could offer to develop in your ministry?

KEY
POINTS

2. CHALLENGE THEM APPROPRIATELY.

Potential leaders need to be challenged, not just taught. Give them a problem to solve. The challenge should be

145

personal, attainable, measurable, and important. Unless a person is stretched, it is impossible to assess his potential.

What are some challenges you could offer potential leaders?

3. INVEST RESOURCES INTO THEM GENEROUSLY.

You'll make a great statement to potential leaders if you generously put resources in their hands. This could be books, ideas, mentors, recordings, or training. A good resource can sustain what is learned at a conference or meeting.

What are some resources you could invest in potential leaders?

4. ALLOW THEM TO ACCOMPANY YOU AND WATCH YOU LEAD.

People do what people see. Let them see you model what you want them to learn. Be an example of people skills, decision making, good planning, and vision casting.

Where are some places you could take potential leaders to watch you at work?

5. IDENTIFY THEIR STRENGTHS AND ENCOURAGE THEM OFTEN.

Locate their God-given gifts and encourage them to lead from those gifts. Affirm what you see. Encouragement is the oxygen of the soul.

How can you identify talents in potential leaders and affirm them?

6. GIVE THEM RESPONSIBILITY AND AUTHORITY FOR SOME TASK.

Potential leaders eventually must be given responsibility for a task; they must do more than follow you. Give them ownership of a task and the authority to do it.

What are some responsibilities you could delegate to potential leaders?

7. EVALUATE THEM ON A REGULAR BASIS.

Balance your expectation with your inspection. Potential leaders must hear your assessment of their growth and their progress on the job. Try this checklist:

- Are they doing what is expected?
- Are they learning while they are doing?
- Are they effective with people?
- Are they ready for new challenges?

ASSESSMENT: *Answer the questions from the list above. Where are you strong? Where are you weak?*

ACTION PLAN

_____

_____

_____

_____

_____

_____

APPLICATION: *Who are some potential leaders you will begin developing?*

_____

_____

_____

_____

_____

Characteristics of a Giant Killer

Lesson 12

How to Handle Your Greatest Leadership Challenges

Then David said to the Philistine, "You come to me with a sword, a spear, and a javelin, but I come to you in the name of the LORD of hosts . . . This day the LORD will deliver you up into my hands, and . . . all the earth may know that there is a God in Israel."
(1 Sam. 17:45–46 NASB)

BIBLICAL BASIS

Giant Truths and Giants in Life

- **Every "giant" introduces me to MYSELF.**

    A crisis doesn't make us, it only reveals what we already are. Negative situations or challenges only uncover what is inside a leader.

- **People who reach "giant positions" have DEFEATED giants.**

    No team or person has ever achieved greatness without facing a giant obstacle. In a 1962 study entitled "Cradles of Eminence," researchers found one common thread running through all the outstanding lives they studied. Almost all of them had to overcome very difficult obstacles in order to become who they were.

- **Giants are often TOOLS God uses to shape us for bigger opportunities.**

  Once young David knocked down Goliath, most people could see he was being prepared for national leadership.

List some "giants" in your life:

_____

_____

_____

_____

Ten Characteristics of a Giant Killer (1 Sam. 17)

1. Giant killers don't BEGIN as giant killers (vv. 14–24).

When war broke out between the Philistines and the Israelites, David was young. He was a musician, and he was a shepherd. While his brothers served as soldiers, David became an errand-boy for his dad, carrying food and checking up on them. He found the soldiers dressed for battle but never engaging the enemy. Goliath wouldn't go away; for forty days, he kept coming back saying the same thing.

Observations on David and the soldiers:

- David was faithful in every one of his small tasks.

- The army was unfaithful in their very large task.

2. Giant killers see the potential REWARD if they defeat the giant (vv. 25–27).

The majority of the crowd sees the obstacles; only a few see the objectives. What separates the fruitful leader from the unfruitful one is this: fruitful leaders see the impact and reward for taking a risk, and they take it. For others, the risk seems too high. On the day David faced Goliath, everyone had the same opportunity:

- The army saw Goliath.

- David saw God.

- The army saw the problem.

- David saw the potential.

We cannot evaluate a situation in terms of what we see. What is observable is real, but it is not the ultimate reality. Behind what we see is an all-powerful, loving God, and we must remind ourselves of this reality.

3. Giant killers don't listen to doubting CRITICS (vv. 28–33, 41–44).

EXAMINE
THE
WORD

You can easily determine the caliber of a person by the amount of opposition it takes to discourage him. Like David, we must do three things to handle critics:

- We must get past our Eliabs. (They intimidate us emotionally.)

153

- We must get past our Sauls. (They intimidate us with their position.)
- We must get past our Goliaths. (They intimidate us with their ability.)

David's critics said things like: "You don't belong here." "You're too young." "You are full of pride." "You are inexperienced." It was tough because the criticism was continual. It came from respectable people in his life; they questioned his motives and abilities. Remember, everyone who has never killed a giant will tell you it is impossible.

4. Giant killers are not overwhelmed by the CHALLENGE (v. 32).

The Israelite army cowered in fear. They had legitimate reasons for their anxiety. Goliath was the most fierce and powerful opponent they had ever seen. But David wanted to know who it was that defied the armies of the living God. The army saw Goliath as too big to hit. David saw him as too big to miss. We can get overwhelmed when we get in David's situation:

- Our giants have a reputation.
- Our giants continually confront us.
- Our giants keep defeating us psychologically.
- Others on our side are afraid.
- We come together and never deal with the giant.
- Our leader is afraid of the giant.

Why wasn't David overwhelmed?

- His passion was for God to be honored.
- His desire was for the reward.
- His confidence was in God to be his strength.

5. Giant killers build upon past SUCCESSES (vv. 34–37).

David's confidence was based on God's protection in successful encounters with a lion and a bear. He reminded himself and the people of the faithfulness of God.

List an accomplishment in your life that brought you a sense of pride:

_____

_____

It likely involved a challenge. You probably felt some self-doubt, but you eventually gave it your total commitment. After the challenge is over, we often forget the initial self-doubt we felt, but when we remind ourselves of God's faithfulness we can defeat self-doubt in the future.

6. Giant killers CONVINCE others they will be successful (v. 37).

What you believe means more than anything else in tough situations: more than what you earn, more than where you live, more than your social position, and more than what anyone else may think about you. Jesus said, "According to your faith let be it to you" (Matthew 9:29 NKJV).

Self-confidence causes others to believe in you. God-confidence causes others to believe in God. Saul eventually said to David, "Go and may the Lord be with you."

7. Giant killers don't try to be SOMEONE ELSE (vv. 38–40).

King Saul offered David his own armor and weapons. David tried them on out of courtesy, but realized they didn't fit who he was. Often you will find yourself in this same kind of situation:

- During a crisis, people will try to make you like them.

- You will never defeat the giants in your life with fleshly weapons.

- God only expects us to use what we have in overcoming our giants.

8. Giant killers face the challenge with a higher PURPOSE (vv. 45–47).

David saw this challenge as being more than just a battle with a nine-foot-tall guy. He faced it with a higher purpose. David ran to the battle so that the world would know the Lord of hosts. He saw it as an enemy without a covenant with the living God versus a man who did have a covenant and who represented Him. It was a statement of things to come of God's great power.

"The real test of a man is not when he plays the role that he wants for himself, but when he plays the role destiny has for him." —Bob Buford

The Power of a Higher Purpose

- Noah could overcome the scoffing of people because he had a purpose.

- Abraham could leave his home for a new land because he had a purpose.

KEY POINTS

156

- Joseph had strength to endure a dark prison because he had a dream.

- Daniel could sleep in a lions' den because he clung to a higher purpose.

- The three Hebrew men could enter a furnace because they had a purpose.

- John the Baptist could decrease in popularity because he had a purpose.

- Stephen preached and died for an unpopular gospel because of purpose.

- Paul endured torture, slander, and shipwreck because he had a purpose.

- Jesus, our example, endured the cross because of His higher purpose: to seek and to save the lost!

9. Giant killers are eager to WIN (v. 48).

The first step to solving any problem is to begin. Overcomers are inspired by a challenge and are passionate to win the victory. David didn't walk toward Goliath—he ran! You can judge the size of a person by the size of the problem they are willing to face.

10. Giant killers take those around them to a HIGHER level (vv. 49–52).

The first sign of a crisis is when you have a major problem and no one tries to help you solve it. Once David solved the problem of Goliath, the armies of Israel ran to chase down the rest of the Philistine army. They won the battle that day but were able to win only because David paved the way for them.

NOTES

ACTION PLAN

ASSESSMENT: *What are the "giants" you face today?*

_____

_____

_____

_____

APPLICATION: *What will be your initial steps to conquer those giants?*

_____

_____

_____

_____

About the Authors

Dr. John Hull
President/CEO, EQUIP.

A frequent speaker at local churches and global outreach events, Hull regularly provides leadership training to audiences in Asia, Europe, the Middle East and Far East, Africa, and the Americas.

Prior to his work with EQUIP, Hull served congregations in the United States and Canada, most recently as Senior Pastor of Peoples Church in Toronto. He earned a degree in journalism and telecommunications from the University of Georgia, a Master of Divinity degree from Liberty Baptist Theological Seminary, and a Doctor of Ministry degree from Gordon-Conwell Theological Seminary.

EQUIP's founder, John Maxwell, says: "John Hull's vast relationships in the evangelical world add tremendous value to EQUIP's on-going mission of training leaders worldwide. He's without question a valued member of my inner circle."

Monthly Hull hosts *"The Global Stage,"* where he interviews leaders from around the world who assist EQUIP in training and resourcing hundreds of thousands of leaders worldwide. *Leadership Moment*, a radio ministry of EQUIP, is also hosted by Hull as well as the EQUIP *President's Forum*, which provides mentoring forums for emerging pastors across the United States twice a year.

Hull has written numerous magazine articles and co-authored *Pivotal Praying* with Tim Elmore. He also writes a bi-monthly column on leadership and global concerns for Christianworkplace.com. John resides in Atlanta with his wife, Sharon, and two children, Andy and Mary Alice.

Dr. Doug Carter
Senior Vice President, EQUIP.

Doug Carter has served as Senior Vice President at EQUIP. since 1996. Previously, Doug and his wife, Winnie, served as missionaries to Native Americans for more than sixteen years. In 1980, Dr. Carter became president of Circleville Bible College where he served nine years, helping prepare men and women for Christian service.

From 1989 until he joined EQUIP. in 1996, Carter served as Vice President of World Gospel Mission, an interdenominational mission agency with 330 career missionaries sharing the gospel in twenty-four nations. He is an outstanding communicator who has ministered in more than eighty nations worldwide.

Carter is the author of *Big Picture People*, a vital resource for Christians who want to press beyond mediocrity and rise to excellence in their faith. He has also written booklets about ministry funding, partnership, and biblical stewardship.

Carter represents EQUIP. in churches and conferences across America and teaches in EQUIP. leadership conferences around the world. He also serves on the boards of several other Christian organizations. Doug and Winnie reside in Atlanta. They are the parents of three children—Angie, Eric, and Jason.

Dr. Tim Elmore
Founder and President, Growing Leaders, Inc.

Tim is the Founder and President of Growing Leaders (www.growingleaders.com), a non-profit organization created to develop emerging leaders. Through Growing Leaders, he and his team are equipping middle-school, high-school, and college students on hundreds of campuses in the U.S. and around the world. Tim has also equipped leaders in corporations such as Chick-fil-A, HomeBanc, Gold Kist, and Home and Garden Party. He has served as Vice President of Leadership Development at EQUIP., training leaders internationally in forty countries. He is currently a Senior Associate with EQUIP..

Since 1979, Tim has served in corporate, non-profit, and church environments. He received his bachelors degree from Oral Roberts University, and his masters and doctorate degrees from Azusa Pacific University. Since 1983, Tim has served under and been mentored by Dr. John Maxwell, leadership author and speaker. Tim has authored numerous books, including the best-selling *Habitudes: Images that Form Leadership Habits & Attitudes* and *Nurturing the Leader Within Your Child*. Along with leadership, Tim has a passion for mentoring and continually mentors leaders from around the country each year. He has written *Mentoring: How to Invest Your Life in Others*.

Tim lives in Atlanta with his wife, Pam, and two children, Bethany and Jonathan.

making a difference for churches from coast to coast

INJOY Stewardship Services was founded by **John C. Maxwell** *to help churches accelerate their growth and achieve their goals in the areas of leadership and stewardship. Dr. Maxwell's world-class team of ISS consultants and specialists have partnered with* **4,000 churches** *to raise over* **$4 billion** *for ministry projects.*

Inspired by a legendary leader and guided by visionary ideals, ISS is truly making a difference in churches nationwide. ISS can make a lasting difference in your church, too.

legendary leadership.
visionary stewardship.
innovative partnership.

"I always expected ISS to have a major influence on churches and church leaders, but the actual impact is above and beyond all expectations. What a joy it is to see how ISS is making a difference in thousands of churches and millions of lives."

John C. Maxwell

For more information *(and some valuable resources)*, call ISS toll-free today at
1.800.333.6509
www.injoystewardship.com

C ONTINUE DEVELOPING your own essential leadership skills with one of these great workbooks from one of the world's most recognized leadership experts— John Maxwell.

Published by
THOMAS NELSON
Since 1798
www.thomasnelson.com

BOOKS BY DR. JOHN C. MAXWELL
CAN TEACH YOU HOW TO BE A REAL SUCCESS

RELATIONSHIPS
Becoming a Person of Influence
Relationships 101
The Treasure of a Friend
25 Ways to Win with People
Winning with People

EQUIPPING
Developing the Leaders Around You
Equipping 101
Partners in Prayer
The 17 Essential Qualities of a Team Player
The 17 Indisputable Laws of Teamwork
Success One Day at a Time
Teamwork Makes the Dream Work
Your Road Map for Success

ATTITUDE
Attitude 101
The Difference Maker
Failing Forward
The Journey from Success to Significance
Living at the Next Level
The Winning Attitude
Your Bridge to a Better Future

LEADERSHIP
Developing the Leader Within You
Developing the Leader Within You Workbook
Leadership 101
The Right to Lead
The 360 Degree Leader
The 21 Indispensable Qualities of a Leader
The 21 Irrefutable Laws of Leadership
The 21 Most Powerful Minutes in a Leader's Day